Timeless W

AIDAN MORAN is a Professor of Psychology and Director of the Psychology Research Laboratory in the School of Psychology, UCD Dublin. A Fulbright Scholar, his research interests include cognitive psychology (mental imagery, critical thinking) and sport psychology (concentration, eye-tracking, expertise). He has written six books, many book-chapters and published extensively in leading journals. Among his books are *The Psychology of Concentration in Sport Performers: A Cognitive Analysis* (Psychology Press, 1996*), Managing Your Own Learning at University: A Practical Guide* (UCD Press, 2000), *Sport Psychology: Contemporary Themes* (Palgrave Macmillan, 2004, with David Lavallee, John Kremer and Mark Williams) and *Sport and Exercise Psychology: A Critical Introduction* (2004, Psychology Press/Routledge).

MICHAEL O'CONNELL is senior lecturer in social psychology at UCD Dublin. His research interests are in the area of group beliefs and attitudes, media representations, the psychology of crime, and economic psychology. He has published articles and chapters in leading journals and books, and co-edited books: *Crime and Poverty in Ireland* (Round Hall, Sweet and Maxwell, with Ivana Bacik in 1998) and *Cultivating Pluralism* (Oak Tree Press, with Malcolm MacLachlan in 2000), and authored *Changed Utterly* (Liffey Press, 2001) as well as *Right-wing Ireland?* (Liffey Press, 2003).

Timeless Wisdom

What Irish Proverbs Tell Us About Ourselves

AIDAN MORAN
MICHAEL O'CONNELL

University College Dublin Press
Preas Choláiste Ollscoile Bhaile Átha Cliath

First published 2006 by
UNIVERSITY COLLEGE DUBLIN PRESS
Newman House, 86 St Stephen's Green,
Dublin 2, Ireland
www.ucdpress.ie

ISBN 978-1-904558-81-1

CIP data available
from the British Library

Typeset in France in Ehrhardt by
Elaine Burberry
Text design by Lyn Davies
Printed in England on acid-free paper by
Antony Rowe Ltd, Chippenham, Wiltshire

Contents

Illustrations

Acknowledgements

The idea for this book grew out of a simple observation. Although Irish proverbs contain a wealth of insights into, and advice about, human nature, no published attempt has been made as yet to analyse their psychological significance. In writing this book, we attempted not only to fill this gap in the literature but also to challenge readers to explore these proverbs for themselves.

If it is true that 'Tosach maith leath na hoibre' ('A good start is half the work'), we were very fortunate in the encouragement, advice and support for this project that we received at the outset from a number of colleagues, friends and family members. In short, this book would not have been possible without the help of many people. To begin with, we wish to acknowledge gratefully the unstinting support supplied by Ms Barbara Mennell (Executive Editor, UCD Press) during the various stages of our writing. We are also indebted to Dr Tina Hickey (UCD School of Psychology) for her enthusiasm, translation skills and for writing such a scholarly foreword to our work. We wish to thank Dr Fionnuala Carson-Williams (Linen Hall Library, Belfast) for her initial suggestions about the direction of the book and also Professor Patricia Lysaght (UCD School of Irish, Celtic Studies, Irish Folklore and Linguistics) for her constructive comments on a section of the draft manuscript. Our indexer, Julitta Clancy, also gave us invaluable help. Our research on the identification and analysis of relevant source material was facilitated greatly by the expertise, time and generosity of Ms Ursula Byrne (Library) and Ms Patricia Moloney (Folklore Archive). Other scholars who offered valuable suggestions in this regard include Professor Bo Almqvist, Criostóir MacCarthaigh and Bairbre Ní Fhloinn (all of the UCD School of Irish, Celtic Studies, Irish Folklore and

Linguistics), Dr Brendan McWilliams, and Dr Fran O'Rourke (UCD School of Philosophy). We are also very thankful to Mr Philip Harvey (Campus Bookshop) for the personal interest which he has shown in this book from its inception. We are also grateful to the National University of Ireland for a grant to facilitate publication of this monograph. Finally, we wish to thank our wives (Angela and Pauline), children (Kevin, Saul, Elliot and Charlie) and families for their love and support at all times. Through them, we discovered the wisdom of the saying 'Ar scáth a chéile a mhaireann na daoine' ('People live under each other's protection').

AIDAN MORAN
MICHAEL O'CONNELL
Dublin, March 2006

Foreword

TINA HICKEY

Proverbs offer us a wealth of wisdom wrapped up in wit. Francis Bacon declared that 'the genius, wit and spirit of a nation are discovered in its proverbs'. One indication of the longevity of proverbs comes from the Old Testament, since proverbs have a respected place in Judeo-Christian teaching. Solomon wrote the Book of Proverbs to help his followers to 'know wisdom and discipline, to discern the sayings of understanding, to receive the discipline that gives insight, righteousness and judgment and uprightness, to give to the inexperienced ones shrewdness, to a young man knowledge and thinking ability' (Proverbs 1: 2–4). His method was to define wisdom by example, often contrasting the wise man's and the fool's way of working. He gave counsel on themes such as striving for spirituality, avoiding anger and strife, keeping our own counsel and valuing hard work. The person who can apply the values of Solomon's proverbs achieves wisdom, while the fool is his antithesis, for example: 'He that gathereth in summer is a wise son: but he that sleepeth in harvest is a son that causeth shame' (Proverbs 10: 5). The vividness of the imagery used helps us to relate still to the timeless truths present in biblical proverbs such as: 'Better a dinner of herbs where love is, than a stalled ox and hatred therewith.' (Proverbs 15: 17)

Moving several thousand years and miles closer to home, we find that Irish proverbs provide us with a unique insight into the spirit of our own forebears, showing us that, while our everyday life now differs radically from theirs, the human dilemmas we face in love, work, death and money, to name but a few, are very similar to those they faced also. Many Irish adults whose school-learned Irish has long rusted and faded away are able to rustle up a proverb such as 'níl aon tinteán mar do thinteán féin' ('there's no place like home') or 'aithníonn ciaróg ciaróg eile' ('one beetle recognises another one' or 'it takes one to know one') or 'tír gan teanga tír gan anam' (a country without a language is a country without a soul') from the dim recesses of their memory. This shows us one of the most valuable attributes of proverbs: their high memorability. It is this feature, in conjunction with the insight they offer into the culture that coined them, that makes them a valuable tool in the second language classroom. They can illustrate a grammatical point neatly and linger on in learners' memories as a template for future use of that construction. Learning proverbs also helps enrich children's mother-tongue skills, since they require abstract thought and interpretation in order to discern their hidden meaning.

Proverbs retain a certain ceremonial presence in modern texts such as diaries and calendars, and are often linked with the 'thought for the day' school of inspirational writing. We may take them for granted in these contexts or on occasion they may leap out at us as apposite contributions to our current preoccupations. I found myself recently in a spirited discussion of proverbs in a café in Dingle as we discussed the Irish proverbs printed on the bags of sugar supplied with our coffee; the one that drew most heated debate among a group of women was the cynical 'níl leigheas ar an ngrá ach pósadh' (there is no cure for love but marriage)!

Despite the ceremonial role we give to proverbs in our diaries, calendars and formal speeches, concern has been raised that the casual citation of proverbs has suffered significant decline in contemporary life. Here we are helped greatly by developments in Corpus Linguistics that allow examination of the actual use of proverbs in vast corpora of written and spoken language. It appears that news of the death of proverbs has been greatly exaggerated and that they seem to be a strand still in the fabric of the language we speak and write. Studies of the occurrence of proverbial language in data from actual use show that, while we may not quote them as reverentially in their entirety as our predecessors did in writing, nevertheless we frequently quote excerpts from them, such as 'the early bird, I see!' and 'a stitch in time you know' or we playfully alter them to make our point more forcefully, or to sell our product more wittily. Such partial quotation and alteration can work only if we assume that our listeners and readers know and understand the underlying proverb, allowing us to tap into a reservoir of shared knowledge of the proverbs of our culture. The clearest illustration of this is the communication breakdown that occurs when a second language speaker tries to quote from a proverb by translating it directly, and cannot then rely on his or her listeners' shared knowledge of that proverb, since so many proverbs need to be matched for message in another language, rather than translated word for word.

Psychologists have long shown an interest in how we learn and use proverbs. The development of the ability to understand proverbs has attracted significant research, because it is thought that this ability is intimately connected with higher-order cognitive abilities. Research on proverb interpretation and use offers us an insight into how normal and dysfunctional individuals think – in fact, proverb interpretation may be used in assessing for schizophrenia. Proverbs are used in psychotherapy as aids in changing habitual ways of thinking and behaving, because their conciseness and memorability help clients to 'consult' them easily.

However, as Hernardi and Steen (1999) note, the mental and social structures underlying proverbs have only relatively recently begun to be explored. They conjure up an apt image of a campsite where anthropologically trained folklorists and literary scholars have now been joined by cognitive linguists and psychologists to discuss proverbial discourse. Making an especially valuable contribution to that campfire debate is this work by Aidan Moran and Michael O'Connell in which they attempt to tease out the information about the mental and social structures to be found in Irish proverbs in particular. Moran and O'Connell take us beyond the specialist analysis of individual proverbs and their occurrence in different languages and eras as carried out by paremiologists (or scholars of proverbs), and present us with a detailed examination of Irish proverbs and the insights into cultural knowledge contained in them. They address the often contradictory advice found in proverbs from a psychological point of view, and explore the reasons why proverbs with opposite meanings can *both* be true, in different contexts.

Most importantly, by applying this analysis to proverbs in Irish in particular, they offer an exploration of the cultural insights contained in them, and the changes in Irish society over the period since many of these proverbs were coined. These proverbs are, in fact, the preserved butterflies of long-gone summers, impaled in our language as a result of their memorability and witty commentary on universal concerns of human nature, bringing colour to our reflections on the daily dilemmas of our existence. Quoting a proverb allows us to sum up our view of a situation succinctly, and simultaneously link it to our shared cultural knowledge. How more appropriately, then, to conclude here than to add: 'molann an obair na fir' ('the work praises the men')!

Psychology and the Study of Proverbs

Many people rely on 'common sense', or an invisible web of informal beliefs and shared cultural knowledge, in their efforts to understand everyday events and to explain other people's behaviour. Central to our reservoir of inherited folk wisdom is the 'proverb' – a pithy and memorable metaphorical saying which is usually transmitted orally and which is alleged to embody some general truth or wisdom. For example, from our earliest days we are advised by our elders to avoid forming hasty impressions of others because 'you can never judge a book by its cover' (or did you do just that in opening this book?).

Although the usage of such figurative expressions for didactic purposes has declined over the past few centuries, proverbial wisdom is still widely evident in popular culture today. By way of illustration, in the late 1980s, almost 6,000 proverbs were collected from sources such as political speeches, song lyrics, newspaper headlines, advertising slogans and book titles (Whiting, 1989). One reason for the enduring appeal of proverbs is that they appear to offer succinct and memorable insights into universal aspects of human behaviour (Williams, 2003) – insights which can be applied flexibly to a host of everyday emotions and experiences such as friendship, love, health, happiness and success. In short, proverbial maxims provide a practical guide to the problems of life. But what exactly is a proverb? Are the wit and wisdom of proverbs 'true' in the sense that they provide accurate insights into people's behaviour and experience? What types of psychological research have been conducted on them? The purpose of this chapter is to explore the nature, definition and significance of proverbs.

DEFINING THE PROVERB

The issue of definition provides a fundamental obstacle to the study of the proverb. One eminent paremiologist (that is, student of proverbs), Alan Dundes (1981), has noted that there has been a growth in many questions around the proverb such as the rules governing its usage, its usage in concrete versus idealised situations, its link to national characteristics (covered in greater detail in chapter 2) and even the link between proverb usage and mental agility (see below, p. 9). And yet despite this growth in interest in these and other aspects of proverbs, there has never existed an adequate definition of the concept. That the problem is not unique to proverbs (the same has been said to beset the study of folklore, and elsewhere, indeed, within social psychology, the twentieth century saw an explosion in the study of the concept of 'attitudes' without a formalised agreement of what exactly an attitude comprised) does not make it any less an obstacle to a coherent analysis. It is true to say that formal definitions often emerge at the end of an exhaustive period of study of a particular idea, rather than at the beginning, but the emergence of the definitive definition is still awaited.

Another prominent paremiologist, Professor Archer Taylor, began his major book on proverbs with the comment that, 'The definition of a proverb is too difficult to repay the undertaking. An incommunicable quality tells us this sentence is proverbial and that this one is not' (quoted in Dundes, 1981, p. 44). Yet another scholar of the proverb takes the same point of view although without quite the same pessimist tone: 'happily, no definition is really necessary, since all of us know what a proverb is' (Whiting, 1952, p. 331). Whiting's own offering of a definition for the proverb, while not false, is not entirely helpful – 'It is usually short, but need not be; it is usually true, but need not be' (quoted in Dundes, 1981, p. 62). More elegant is Cervantes' idea of the proverb as a 'short sentence drawn from long experience'. It was Robert MacAdam (about whom more in chapter 2) who took issue with Lord John Russell's elegant definition of the proverb as 'the wisdom of many, the wit of one' pointing out that many proverbs are neither witty nor wise. He preferred the Irish term 'Sean-Ráite' (Old Sayings). Ridout and Witting (1969), however, identify certain problems with the epigrammatic or dictionary definitions of proverbs. For example, they note that *The Advanced Learner's Dictionary of Current English* defines the proverb as 'a popular short saying with words of advice or warning'. Does this make any widely used saying a proverb? And if popular means 'of the people', then presumably proverbs have to be old since they must have sunk their roots deep into language. But can old proverbs, no longer in widespread usage and therefore not 'popular', still be called proverbs?

Technically, a proverb may be defined as 'a short, generally known sentence that expresses common, traditional and didactic views in a metaphorical and fixed form and which is easily remembered and repeated' (Mieder, 1985, p. 118). In other words, it is a pithy saying that is held to embody some general truth (Knowles, 1997). Remarkably, at least 55 definitions of proverbs have been proposed by scholars in the field. Having reviewed these definitions, Mieder (1993, p. 24) concluded that the proverb was best regarded as a short, generally known sentence 'which contains wisdom, truth, morals and traditional views in a metaphorical, fixed and memorizable form and which is handed down from generation to generation'.

Dundes ambitiously offers a definition based on the structure of the proverb. He argues that it is

3

a traditional propositional statement consisting of at least one descriptive element, a descriptive element consisting of a topic and a comment.
This means that proverbs must have at least two words. Proverbs which
contain a single descriptive element are non-oppositional [e.g., 'boys
will be boys']. Proverbs with two or more descriptive elements may be
either oppositional [e.g. 'man works from sun to sun but woman's work
is never done'] or non-oppositional [e.g., 'like father, like son'] . . .
Proverbs only state problems in contrast to riddles which solve them
(Dundes, 1981, p. 60).

From these various definitions, we can identify three key criteria
of proverbs. Firstly, there is a preference (but not an absolute
requirement) that they should be witty (or creative and novel).
Secondly, they should contain some wisdom, in the sense that
they convey considerable truth value or plausibility. Thirdly, proverbs have to be memorable. (And perhaps in passing, a fourth
key element might be added – the proverb is a traditional expression, i.e. it persists through time.) Although these three criteria
should be equally important, proverb researchers have tended to
emphasise those concerning wit and wisdom over the criterion of
memorability. But the wisdom of proverbs is difficult to assess. Thus
Fergusson (1983, p. vi), in her introduction to the *Penguin Dictionary
of Proverbs*, suggested that although proverbs have to be short,
memorable and deeper than platitudes, 'they do not have to be true!
Folk wisdom is often contradictory . . . Perhaps it is a mistake to
regard proverbs as a source of accumulated wisdom'. And so we learn
that a good proverb need not necessarily be true (see below for
further consideration of the frustrations entailed by this). Similarly,
not all succinct and truthful expressions qualify as proverbs – they
have to be *memorable* as well. For this latter reason, an intriguing structural feature of many proverbs is their use of rhyme
('man proposes, God disposes' or 'when the cat's away, the mice
will play') or alliteration (in the Irish proverb 'aithníonn ciaróg

ciaróg eile' – or 'one beetle recognises another beetle') to enhance memorability.

The wit, wisdom and memorability of most proverbs make them ideal didactic devices by which people can bring a force of authority to bear on what they say. One example of this appeal to received cultural wisdom occurs in the case of advertising (Mieder and Mieder, 1977). Thus the brevity and apparent trustworthiness of proverbial sayings are helpful in consolidating advertising messages. For example, cameras have been sold using the slogan 'Good things come in small packages'. Likewise, hamburgers have been marketed using the phrase 'man does not live by bread alone' and, in a clever transposition of words, watches have been marketed with the slogan 'there is no present like the time'.

Having explained briefly what proverbs are and why they are appealing, let us now consider their functions.

PROVERBS AND THEIR FUNCTIONS

Why analyse proverbs, or indeed folklore more generally? Richard M. Dorson (1972) considered certain reasons why folklore, including proverbs, are of interest to the researcher. First, they give us a sense of the history of a people and their evolution, and the development of their language and ideas. In Soviet Russia, for example, it was considered that folklore provided a sense of the conflict between the classes – rich and poor – in the past, and also offered an aid to understanding the hopes and expectations of the working masses. Influenced by Bronisław Malinowski, anthropologists have been interested in studying the *functions* of proverbs – what role do or did they play? 'Proverbs help settle legal decisions, riddles sharpen wits, myths validate conduct, satirical songs release pent-up hostilities' (Dorson, 1972, p. 21). Psychoanalysts have interpreted myths and rituals as dealing with unacceptable or repressed wishes around sexuality and violence.

5

Researchers in the 1930s were interested in the repetitive elements of much folklore including proverbs and the manner in which this repetition of the same links occurred across different societies. This suggests a strong overlap with the themes of cross-cultural psychology where some writers felt that quite different societies nonetheless had many common elements, and that assessment of the function and role of the proverb across these different societies would bring such similarities to the fore – as well as differences presumably. Both anthropologists and nationalists have been sceptical of seeing any universality within proverbs, instead searching for the idiosyncrasies and specificities of each national set of expressions, with somewhat mixed results as discussed in greater detail in chapter 2. For some, there is a feeling that proverbs and folklore more widely express the sentiment of the real masses of people against the elite with their cosmopolitan interests. Thus by studying proverbs, we get at what the 'real' people, the 'folk', are actually thinking and saying. According to this view, everyday mass culture is distinctive and vibrant but is being crushed by the steamroller of international culture especially via electronic media. We need to collect and categorise every popular piece of 'talk' since in the not too far distant future, one unique product of each society – its proverbs – will gradually disappear. Urbanisation, in particular, has signalled the end of the rich oral tradition of rural life and is gradually replacing it with a functional, but more bland and less colourful language. Of course, the simplest reason for studying proverbs may simply be their appeal, and perhaps the poetic rhythm in particular of the common heroic couplet, such as Pope's, 'To err is human, to forgive divine'. Thus we can study them as a means to an end (understanding a society or group of societies) or as an end in themselves.

Earlier in the chapter, we explained that because of their brevity and memorability, proverbs make ideal slogans. In this regard, proverbs have been studied for their therapeutic value in reminding people to implement and maintain behavioural change. For example,

6

Rogers (1990) investigated the use of slogans and proverbial sayings ('You alone can do it, but you cannot do it alone' or 'The journey of a thousand miles begins with a single step') as therapeutic tools for people suffering from substance addictions. The value of proverbs in this study was twofold. On the one hand, they offered newcomers to the therapeutic process the promise that there *were* answers to the questions which had troubled them before joining the group ('will I be able to help myself?'). On the other hand, they served as rhetorical devices in persuading members who had received therapeutic treatment to adhere to group norms. Interestingly, proverbs proved to be helpful at different stages of the therapeutic journey. Initially, people were given the proverb 'the journey of a thousand miles begins with a single step' to reinforce the view that the community had an answer to the patient's doubts. Later, during the therapeutic stages, proverbs were used as rhetorical strategies to promote social bonding. Finally, at the conclusion of the therapeutic programme, patients were encourages to use proverbs as reminders to transfer what they had learned to real-life situations. Unfortunately, not all researchers are convinced of the merit of proverbial maxims in self-help therapy. Eret (2001) provided a detailed analysis of the proverbial rhetoric used by Anthony Robbins – a well-known American motivational speaker and advocate of self-help psychology. In this critique, Eret (2001) argued that Robbins's message, in exhorting us relentlessly to make more of ourselves so that we can free ourselves from the shackles of materialism, simply trades one form of unattainable ideal for another. Clearly, the naïve or uncritical usage of proverbs can, in certain circumstances, *enslave* rather than empower us. Comprehensive reviews of the nature, origin and implications of the multi-billion dollar, self-help movement in America have been provided recently by McGee (2005) and Salerno (2005).

Proverbs may also provide us with a window on the maturation of children. For many years, developmental psychologists have been interested in the ways in which children's understanding of proverbs change as children developed. For example, Piaget (1969) gave children aged between 9 and 15 years a series of 10 proverbs and asked them to match them with a series of sentences which contained paraphrases of these proverbs. In general, according to Piaget, these children 'did not understand the proverbs in the least' (1969, p. 142) because they lacked the appropriate abstract thinking skills required to decode them. However, this conclusion has been challenged by Pasamanick (1983) who reported that the children in her study (aged between six and nine years) were capable of rudimentary abstract thinking. Regardless of when exactly the capacity for abstract thought emerges, it is clear that proverb comprehension teaches people that there are hidden layers of meaning in spoken language. Interestingly, this idea that language conveys multiple levels of meaning is evident cross-culturally. Thus Arora (1984) pointed out that proverbs often function as tools by which a parent can guide a child's thoughts or actions using an impersonal blend of authority and collective wisdom from the past. To illustrate, the Yoruba tribe use proverbs to mediate the views of the elders to their children. In this way, the parent is not blamed by the child for scolding him or her – the parent is merely an instrument by which the past is channelled to the child. Thus the parents can disassociate themselves from the utterances used and insist that it is tradition itself, not their voices, that speak to the child.

A related type of psychological research on proverbs is concerned with the analysis of people's ability to understand figurative sayings such as 'a rolling stone gathers no moss', 'let sleeping dogs lie' or 'people in glass houses shouldn't throw stones' in an effort to draw conclusions about their psychological functioning. Consider the use of proverb comprehension as a test of abstract thought. The idea here is that if a person can interpret the 'rolling stone . . .' proverb as indicating that someone who moves around too much may not form social attachments rather than simply as a literal statement about stones and moss, then s/he is assumed to be capable of some degree of abstract thought. Based on this logic, tests of proverb comprehension were among the earliest items to be included in intelligence tests and are still evident in the modern versions of these scales (see the Wechsler scales – Matarazzo, 1972). They have also been used to assess mental health (Andreasen, 1977; Gorham, 1956) and brain dysfunction (e.g., Van Lancker, 1990). With regard to mental health, Benjamin (1944) reported that schizophrenic patients had great difficulty in explaining metaphorical thinking such as proverbs. This finding was confirmed in subsequent research on thinking disorders which showed that people with schizophrenia tended to score below the mean in their ability to interpret such proverbs as 'the proof of the pudding is in the eating' or 'let sleeping dogs lie') taken from the Gorham Proverbs Test (Gorham, 1956). With regard to neuropsychology, there is evidence that damage to the frontal lobes of the brain is associated with impairment in people's ability to interpret proverbs (Cummings, 1985). Caution is necessary, however, when evaluating these claims about the value of proverb tests in diagnosing schizophrenia and brain damage. Indeed, the fact that surprisingly little normative data are available on Gorham's (1956) proverbs test renders meaningful comparisons hazardous if not impossible.

Finally, researchers have explored the role of derogatory or pejorative proverbs in fomenting racism and prejudice (Birnbaum, 1971). In these studies, the term 'ethnophaulisms' (Roback, 1944; from the Greek roots meaning 'a national group' and 'to disparage') is used to describe slurs by an ingroup for an outgroup. For example, early Irish immigrants in the US were called 'spuds', 'croppies', 'micks', 'redshanks' and 'teagues' (Mullen, Rozell and Johnson, 2000). In view of such derogatory language, it is not surprising that ethnophaulic proverbs have also arisen. The proverbial phrase 'the only good Indian is a dead Indian' is attributed widely, if erroneously, to the Irish-American general Philip Henry Sheridan (1831–88). This general is alleged to have proclaimed in January 1869 in Fort Cobb that 'the only good Indians I ever saw were dead'. Exploring the

9

origins of this proverb, Mieder (1997) analysed some of the ethno-phaulic sayings which depicted native Americans in a negative fashion. As far back as the 1770s, the phrase 'Indians will be Indians' was used to argue that some people would remain uncivilised no matter what help was provided for them.

DIFFICULTIES AND FRUSTRATIONS
IN STUDYING PROVERBS

Inspired by the challenge of assessing the accuracy of various precepts of common sense, some researchers have tested the validity of proverbial sayings by subjecting their claims to empirical scrutiny. This quest is supported by the discovery that there are similar kinds of proverbs in different languages (Mieder, 1985) – a fact which suggests that proverbs may seek to portray some universal truths about the world. Proverbs thus serve as the starting point for further research. The question faced by researchers is whether or not proverbs provide useful and/or accurate insights into human behaviour. Unfortunately, this question has proved rather difficult to answer because proverbs often provide contradictory advice and predictions (Epstein, 1997; Stanovich, 2004). In fact, the existence of contradictory proverbs has long attracted attention, at least since the Middle Ages. For example, whereas on the one hand, it is alleged that 'absence makes the heart grow fonder', it may also be claimed that 'out of sight, [means] out of mind'. Similarly, although it is said that 'great minds think alike', it is also held that 'fools seldom differ'. Likewise, we are often exhorted to 'look before you leap' – but are advised equally that 'he who hesitates is lost'. Also, although 'two heads are better than one', we are also reminded that 'too many cooks spoil the broth'. Furthermore, if people accept that 'it's better to be safe than sorry', why do they also believe that 'nothing ventured, nothing gained'? And we must acknowledge the classic contradictions between 'opposites attract' and 'birds of a feather flock together'. Likewise, there is a direct conflict between such expressions as 'where there's a will there's a way' and 'you can't have your cake and eat it'. Psychologically, this widespread contradiction is interesting as it may help to explain the appeal and tenacity of proverbs. That is, these proverbs cannot be refuted easily because no matter what transpires, we always have recourse to a contradictory yet equally forceful alternative. As Stanovich (2004, p. 14) concluded, they allow us to have 'an explanation for anything and everything that happens'.

At first glance, the fact that proverbial insights are often contradictory suggests that they may be of little value as informal psychological theories. But this conclusion is questionable for at least two reasons. First, contradiction is not the sole preserve of folk wisdom. Psychological research findings are also frequently at odds with each other. Indeed, researchers are often attracted to a specific topic simply because of opposing theories, findings or predictions around it. Second, the search for universal truth in proverbs seems naïve when one considers that all proverbs are products of a particular time, place and culture. Therefore, proverbs offer contextually bound insights rather than universal truths. We shall return to this point about contextual influences on proverbs below. In passing, we should note that the precepts of common sense change from era to era. As Stanovich (2004) pointed out, almost everyone 'knew' more than a century ago that women should not be allowed to vote and that children with physical and mental disabilities should be locked up in institutions for the rest of their lives. Fortunately, more enlightened beliefs prevail about these issues today.

Despite the preceding problems, a considerable amount of research has been conducted on the degree to which proverbial insights are supported by empirical psychological research evidence. What this research shows is that proverbial wisdom is not consistently accurate in its insights into human behaviour (Rogers, 1990).

For example, on the positive side, it appears to be true that 'confession is good for the soul'. Thus according to Pennebaker (1997), there is evidence that people who engage in regular self-disclosure tend to have superior mental and physical health to people who 'bottle up' their thoughts and feelings. Similarly, consider the proverb 'all work and no play makes Jack a dull boy'. Again, there is evidence (e.g., Knauth, 1996) that people who work long hours may display slower reaction times and less alertness than people who work shorter hours. Perhaps not surprisingly, leisure activities such as physical exercise are associated with improved mood and an enhanced sense of well-being. Unfortunately, there are plenty of examples of research which seem to contradict proverbial truths. For example, 'ignorance is bliss' does not appear to be literally true (Siegelman, 1981). Likewise, the idea that 'familiarity breeds contempt' is challenged by studies which show that people's favourable ratings of stimuli tend to increase with additional exposure to them (Zajonc, 1968). Other proverbs whose insights are supported by psychological research are 'birds of a feather flock together' (which seems to be true as regards mate selection; Cash and Derlega, 1978) and 'first impressions are lasting' (Asch, 1946).

From the preceding evidence, it seems reasonable to conclude that most proverbs are only partly true. But how do we measure 'truth' without taking cultural and contextual factors into account? Gibbs and Beitel (1995) concluded that although many proverbs convey accurate insights into human behaviour, the extent to which any single one is truthful or not depends significantly on contextual factors. As they put it, 'proverbs might best be thought of as neither true nor false but . . . applicable or inapplicable given the situation in which they are instantiated' (1995, p. 135). Interestingly, Teigen (1986) found that people *do* interpret the proverb 'too many cooks spoil the broth' to be true of cognitive tasks and they suggested that its opposite – 'many hands make light work' – was true of manual tasks. Similarly, Furnham (1987) reported that when people refer to close friends, 'absence makes the heart grow fonder' is regarded as being true, whereas for casual acquaintances, 'out of sight, out of mind' is deemed to be true. Likewise, Gibbs and Beitel (1995) observed that while 'beware of Greeks bearing gifts' may be true in the case of strangers, 'never look a gift horse in the mouth' is rated as true when speaking of close friends but not casual acquaintances.

Against this background, what is the analyst to do, faced with regular duplicity, yet great numerical complexity and the dependence on shifting context? Our strategy in this book has been threefold. First, as can be seen above, we have tried to select those proverbs that have had the most resonance with psychology, either because they appear to us to be strangely modern in their approach, chiming in with a recently achieved psychological consensus on a topic. Or alternatively, where they run directly counter to psychological claims, theories and expectations about human behaviour, we have noted and discussed them in greater detail and tried to reflect on reasons for the difference in perspective.

Second, we have in places used a type of frequency analysis; part of the frustrating charm of proverbs, again as noted above, is the regularity with which one will find one proverb asserting one 'truth' and, just as easily, another stating precisely the opposite will come to mind ('many hands make light work', 'too many cooks spoil the broth' etc.). Now sometimes, as we saw, there may be logical reasons for these oppositions (for example, for simple repetitive work, many hands will lighten the work, but for complex decision-making tasks such as cooking an elaborate meal, a single co-ordinator will often be for more effective). But more often, none are apparent. For the research psychologist, looking for the modal or typical case within a given domain is often the best strategy when faced with unreliable single pieces of 'data'.

Third, cross-cultural analysis and comparison of proverbs can also allow us to make reasonable inferences about the psychological role that proverbs can play in different types of societies. Where available, these cross-cultural variations will be included in our analysis. Cross-cultural forms of analyses, intuitively powerful, made a strong impact on psychology only from the 1970s onwards. Inevitably in psychology, where the environment has a strong impact on someone's behaviour, it is easy to mistake the products of that environment for universal 'iron' laws of human development. North America has especially dominated the development of modern psychology and its research; testing the intellectual and predictive models that have been pioneered there in other societies has been a useful corrective to a mono-social outlook. For example, the assumption that people always engage in 'social loafing' (working less hard in a group when their individual output cannot be measured) seems to be confirmed when tested on various age- and social-groups in the USA. However, research in Asian societies show that people often work more productively together, rather than separately. Paradoxically with proverbs, we have seen that the anthropological tendency has been to assume the opposite, that proverbs are nation- or group-specific, while the folklorists have been more likely to take the universal-ist perspective, that is to assume that the same kinds of proverbs, in terms of topics, crop up repeatedly, although obviously how they are actually expressed will vary. Only looking at proverbs across different cultures will allow a resolution of this complex but 'big' question.

There is, however, one further difficulty, or perhaps one should say a frustration, for the authors in approaching the issue of proverbs in a convincing way. As academic psychologists, we are trained and committed to a scientific approach to dealing with all sorts of phenomena, conundrums, questions about human nature and so on. Thus, being a good research psychologist does not mean having necessarily great intuition about the way humans behave.

Neither does it mean that one cannot have theories, hunches, guesses, or indeed intuitions about such matters but that one needs to test such views against available data. The soundness of one's conclusions then is based at least partly (if not mainly) on the quality of the data one has amassed and interrogated. The problem with proverbs is that one cannot be sure if one has collected all the available ones that are in use (there are other problems inherent in the analysis of proverbs of course, see chapter 7). In the course of writing this book, we used a number of collections of proverbs gathered by specialists in the field such as Williams, Gaffney, Partridge and Cashman and are very grateful that these collections were available. However, it is striking how small the overlap between the different collections are; in other words, it is quite rare for precisely the same proverb to crop up more than once. Even where the classic and comprehensive collections of proverbs are appealed to (such as the Irish language collections of An Seabhac, Ó Máille and Ó Muirgheasa), these concerns about capturing all of the possible proverbs are reduced but not extinguished. If each specialist trawls the literature but generates a different set, it strikes the research scientist immediately as a problem related to the *reliability* and *validity* of the data on which we want to base our conclusions – can we be sure that we really have the complete set of proverbs so that our analysis will be meaningful? In fact, we cannot and the reader will have to make his/her own judgements about whether the conclusions we draw are safe.

IN OUR DEFENCE

In a more positive vein, however, psychology and psychologists have shown a marked ability to deal with complex and difficult topics. That proverbs deal with a breadth of issues might have deterred a more purist discipline from searching out patterns inhering in the chaos. But psychological research is notorious for taking on apparently intangible and messy topics like interpersonal attraction, multiple intelligences, or indeed like emotion and memory. Smart thinking, crafty techniques and agreed norms have been used to turn elusive and subtle concepts into recognisable and definable independent variables (inputs) and dependent variables (outputs). Perhaps that is why the media take such an interest in the proceedings of psychology conferences – because the research appears to transform everyday, vague concerns and questions into comprehensible research questions with transparent answers.

Our approach in writing this book has been to try to apply such psychological rigour and insights as are possible in the interpretation of the proverbs we have encountered. Interestingly, our review of the literature concerning proverbs suggests that this approach is rare. Much more commonly, one finds either of two approaches: the first tends to offer a short and general introduction to the nature of proverbs, followed by a listing of proverbs under various headings. The other approach instead takes one, several or at most a thematic group of proverbs and subjects them to extremely detailed, learned and sometimes esoteric analysis. The format of the former category tends to be the short book and of the latter, the specialist chapter in an edited book or the journal article. Given that there are journals dedicated specifically to the topics of folklore and specifically of proverbs (e.g., *De Proverbio*) as well as websites (e.g., perso.wanadoo.fr/proverbes/proverbe.htm) this specialised discourse is inevitable. Professor Wolfgang Mieder, for example, a German expert on proverbs, based at the University of Vermont, and probably the world's leading expert on paremiology, has published over one hundred books on the area.

Our approach, we feel, is a more middle-level one, sandwiched between the 'list' version of many proverbs versus the detailed microanalyses of the few. Examples of this approach are rare, but in essence our hope is to offer a brief analysis of many proverbs. There is of course the risk that we shall generate an analysis that pleases nobody since it is too specialised for the general reader but too all-encompassing for the specialist; those are the risks one takes since we can only write that which we feel offers the best application of our discipline to the topic in hand.

In case the reader thinks that the proverbs are being singled out for special or unusual treatment by squeezing them through an unedifying, undignified and unnecessary over-analysis, the late twentieth century witnessed an explosion of effort by researchers to capture the essence of culture by careful analysis. One of the best-known examples came from Will Wright's *Sixguns and Society* which offered a structural analysis of the genre of the Western film (published in 1975). In this book, he argued that the Western film was a type of 'myth' for modern US society. By 'myth', he intended not that the idea was false but rather the anthropological notion of it serving to provide a model or vision with which people could make sense of their everyday experience. Furthermore, by reading and observing the structure of a particular narrative (in this case, the Western film), people learn themselves how it is they should behave. Wright's interpretation of the Western was that its classic plot shows that 'the way to achieve such human rewards as friendship, respect, dignity is to separate yourself from others and use your strength as an autonomous individual to succor [support/comfort] them. The vengeance variation [of the Western, especially the film *Shane*] shows that the path to respect and love is to separate yourself from others, struggling individually against your many and strong enemies but striving to remember and return to the softer values of marriage and humility' (Wright, 1975, pp. 186–7).

Wright was certainly not alone in his analysis; the 1970s in particular witnessed the blossoming of a period of academic deconstruction of mass culture. The principal or main aim of much of the analysis might be described as separating the manifest from the latent. The manifest is the content we observe, the surface material;

the assumption made by students of the material is that below the surface lies a deeper latent meaning, waiting to be interpreted. A classic example of this kind of approach was offered by Roland Barthes: his interpretation of advertisements differentiated between the 'signifier', that is the physical image of the advertisement (for example one using a photograph of a black French soldier) and the meaning that can be taken from it (that which is 'signified'). At the superficial level the advertisement may evoke images of military power, but at a deeper level and in the context of a time when France's African colonies were in revolt against their imperial master, it may be that the advertisement also signified loyalty of Africa to metropolitan France. Thus its ideological content is signified at a deeper level. Similarly, the image of a meal of steak and chips at one level is simply that – the image of a traditional meal. But for a typical Frenchman, it may conjure up a deeper meaning behind the first – the very concept of Frenchness, of enjoying one's 'steack et frites'. What the analyses of Wright and Barthes have in common is the idea that one can look behind mass culture and read latent, more fundamental meanings there with careful study.

So attempting to subject a widespread cultural phenomenon to careful scrutiny and evaluation is not an odd project. It is, however, a difficult one and this arises from the very nature of proverbs themselves; they are both simpler and more complex at the same time than other cultural products. Although individual proverbs themselves may become reasonably fixed or crystallised, the frequency and circumstances of their usage is almost impossible to ascertain. Unlike the film, advertisement, painting or book which all have a physical record, the vast bulk of language in everyday usage goes unrecorded. That which is recorded is more likely to involve ritual or include the language of elites and therefore not to be representative of everyday, especially rural communication, of the people. Proverbs are extremely numerous; they are likely to spread like diseases and in much the same manner, based on contact so that isolated areas may retain older forms long after they have disappeared in regions with greater penetration. But they are also usually problematically simple – they say exactly what they say![1]

---

1   There may not be an underlying or deeper meaning 'signified' beyond what is reasonably clear; however, in the chapter on food and drink, a few exceptions to this rule are listed, where the proverb seems to be about food but is really about something else, for example 'the crab tree has a sweet blossom', the implication being that a pretty façade can disguise a bitterness below.

2

Proverbs and Irish Society

INTRODUCTION

Like many nationalities with a rich linguistic heritage, Irish people
are generally proud of their past and largely respectful of the wisdom
and traditions that it has spawned. This respect is deep-rooted and
widely evident. To illustrate, consider the reverence for 'pastness'
that is epitomised by the saying 'Ná déan nós is ná bris nós' or 'Don't
make a custom or don't break a custom'. Clearly, the injunction here
is not to tamper with tradition because it is a repository of folk wisdom. In Ireland, the proverbial insights enshrined in 'seanfhocail'
(literally translated as 'old words') are sometimes held to provide a
glimpse of eternal verities – especially as they appear to speak with
the authority of tradition. For example, one way of describing a
person's death in Irish is to say that s/he is 'in the place of truth
now' – 'tá sé/sí in áit na fírinne anois'. In addition, a glance at Irish
history shows that proverbs have been quoted at pivotal points in the
country's economic development. Fionnuala Williams, the Irish
proverbs scholar, noted that Seán Lemass, the former Taoiseach,
used a vivid maritime proverb in the late 1960s (namely, 'A rising
tide lifts all boats') when assessing the significance of the mini-boom
of that era. Of course, proverbs can also be used to stoke up national
fervour (see Raymond, 1956) and enmity between in-groups and
their rivals (see also chapter 8). Another indication of Irish people's
respect for traditional wisdom comes from the fact that proverbial

expressions of it are represented in a remarkable variety of cultural artefacts in contemporary Irish society. They are evident not only in books (e.g., Kelly, 1996) and CDs (e.g., Fios Feasa, 1998) but also in pocket diaries (e.g., Bord na Gaeilge UCD's Dialann 2006), educational flashcards (see the Glór na nGael series produced by Comhdháil Náisúnta na Gaeilge), holiday postcards, on matchboxes (see the Cara matches produced by Maguire & Paterson) and even on sachets of condiments (see Gem white sugar). Taken together, these various strands of evidence attest to the popularity of proverbial wisdom among Irish people of all ages.

But how 'Irish' are these so-called 'Irish proverbs'? What are the distinctive features of these traditional figurative expressions and where have they been collected? Can they shed any light on the elusive nature of the Irish psyche or 'national character'? And how can proverbial insights retain their freshness and relevance in a rapidly changing Irish society, where the very survival of the Irish language is under threat every year? The purpose of the present chapter is to address these questions.

In order to facilitate these objectives, the chapter is organised as follows. To begin with, we shall explore the transmission and characteristics of Irish proverbs. After that, we shall provide a brief sketch of their psychological significance. Next, we shall consider how such proverbs have been collected. Then, we shall tackle the question of whether or not proverbs help us to understand certain aspects of the Irish identity. In the next section, we examine the relevance of proverbs in a changing Irish society. Finally, we shall explore the dynamic nature of expressions of wisdom by mentioning the rise of 'anti-proverbs'.

Ná déan nós is ná bris nós (Don't make a custom or don't break a custom). Station Mass in Castlegal County Sligo.

IRISH PROVERBS: TRANSMISSION
AND CHARACTERISTICS

In chapter 1, we explored the nature and functions of proverbs and examined some of the issues raised by studying them. But how is their wisdom transmitted from one generation to the next? One way in which this may occur is through parental guidance. A good example of how respect for 'seanfhocail' can be inculcated in children comes from MacCon Iomaire (1999). Specifically, he recalls how, as a boy growing up in Connemara, he was guided by his mother to place a clutch of eggs under a brooding hen. While he waited three weeks for the eggs to hatch, his mother taught him the literal meaning of the expression 'Ná comhair do chuid sicíní go dtaga siad amach' or 'Don't count your chickens until they are hatched'. This charming incident shows how proverbial wisdom permeated people's lives in Ireland before the advent of the television era. It also highlights the paradox whereby a figurative expression (about counting one's chickens) can be taught to a child in a concrete manner. Interestingly, over time, MacCon Iomaire began to realise that wise sayings were not uttered solely or exclusively by his mother but could be heard in conversations between members of his community – especially among the salutations of people as they stopped to pass the time of day with each other. Incidentally, Irish proverbs caution people to consider carefully the credibility of their advisers. For example, the well-known expression 'is maith an t-iománaí an té a bhíonn ar an gclaí' (or 'he is a good hurler who sits on the ditch') warns us to be on our guard against unsolicited advice from people who have little personal experience of the problem or situation on which they are pontificating. A similar disdain for certain kinds of verbal support is evident in the expression 'Is maith comhairle ach is fearr cabhair' ('advice is good but help is better').

Although Irish proverbs have few *unique* features, they display at least three prominent characteristics. First, a common format of

Irish proverbs is the 'triad' – a figurative expression in which three things are grouped together for the purposes of comparison and illumination (see chapter 8 for a detailed discussion of these expressions). Many of these triads contain witty observations culminating in an amusing if sexist climax in the third item (Kelly, 1996). Consider 'na trí nithe is géire ar bith: Súil circe ndiaidh gráinne, súil gabha i nidiaidh tairne agus súil caillí i ndiaidh bean a mic' (The three sharpest things on earth: A hen's eye after a grain, a blacksmith's eye after a nail and an old woman's eye after her son's wife'). This style of triads dates back at least as far as the ninth century. For example, there are 'trí uara tairiset fri traig ocus fri tuile: uair gene, uair choimpearta, uair scartha anma duine' ('three times that stay not for ebbtide nor for flood: the time of birth, the time of conception, the time the soul departs') (Williams, 2003). Similarly, consider a triad describing the three things that are the most difficult to understand: 'Na trí ruda is deacra do thuiscint san domhan – inntleacht na mban, obair na mbeach, teacht is imeacht na taoide' – 'the mind of a woman, the labour of the bees, the ebb and flow of the tide' (Flanagan, 1995, p. 110). Many of these triads emphasis the theme that women are impossible to understand, being fickle and untrustworthy. Even if one does understand a woman, she is not to be trusted: 'Trí nithe nach buan – bó bhán, bean bhreadh, tigh ar árd' ('three things that are not lasting – a white cow, a handsome woman, a house on a height'). Triads also apply to the problem of alcohol abuse. Thus 'trí bhua an ólacháin: maidin bhrónach, cóta salach, pócaí folamha' ('three faults of drink are a sorrowful morning, a dirty coat and an empty pocket') (Williams, 1992, p. 24). See chapter 8 for a fuller discussion of this unusual triadic structural aspect of Irish proverbs.

A second characteristic feature of many Irish proverbs is the fact that they use a variety of stylistic devices to convey their message and to enhance its memorability. Typical of such devices are images ('Ní are leathchois a thánaig Pádraig go hÉirinn' – 'St Patrick did not come to Ireland on one leg', or more figuratively, ' a bird never flew on one wing'; Partridge, 1978), rhymes ('Ní huasal ná íseal ach thuas seal agus thíos seal' – 'It is not a matter of upper or lower class but of being up for a while and down for a while'; MacCon Iomaire, 1999), and a form of alliteration called *uaim* whereby similar sounds are repeated at the beginning of successive words in order to enhance their memorability (Partridge, 1978). For example, 'Is binn béal ina thost' or 'Silence is golden'. Other examples of this kind are 'Is minic ciúin cionntach' (or 'the silent one is often the guilty one') and 'Más mall is díreach díoltas Dé' (or 'the vengeance of God is direct, even if it is slow').

The third characteristic of many Irish proverbs is that they refer to animals in their analysis of human traits (MacCon Iomaire, 1999). For example, selfish people are compared to cats (see 'Ar mhaithe leis féin a dheineann an cat crónán' – 'A cat purrs for himself'; Williams, 1992, p. 36), people of limited intelligence are compared to donkeys and hard-working people to horses. Another animal proverb suggests that 'Far from home the lapwing calls' ('Is fada ó bhaile a labhraíonn an pilibín'). The message here is that lapwings, like many other birds that nest on the ground, try to lure people away from their young by crying strongly to set a false trail. Metaphorically, this proverb expresses the idea that people often mislead others by saying things that they do not really mean.

SIGNIFICANCE OF IRISH PROVERBS

Many Irish proverbs have a significant truth-value in the sense described in chapter 1 – namely, agreement with research findings from psychology. Here are a number of sayings whose wisdom is readily supported by relevant research:

- 'Ní mar a síltear a bítear' ('things are not always as they appear') – acknowledgement of the role of subjective perception in interpreting everyday events and experiences (Fios Feasa, 1998)

- 'Ocht n-amharc, ocht gcuimhne' ('eight views, eight recollections') – a recognition that people vary from each other in their recall of the same event (Flanagan, 1995, p. 82)

- 'An rud nach éigin aoibhinn' ('that which is not necessary is pleasant') – awareness that people often distract themselves by tackling pleasant but unnecessary tasks rather than urgent yet more demanding ones (Flanagan, 1995, p. 83)

- 'Cuinnidh an cnámh is leanfaidh an madra thú' ('keep hold of the bone and the dog will follow you') – the suggestion that rewards are powerful influences in changing human or animal behaviour (Flanagan, 1995, p. 28)

- 'Is maith an scáthán súil charad' ('the eye of a friend is a good looking-glass') – which conveys the idea that a true friend will give honest advice (Flanagan, 1995, p. 48)

- 'An nídh a chíonn an leanbh,'se a ghnidh an leanbh' ('what the child sees, s/he does') – acknowledgement that children learn from observation of what others do rather than from what such people say (Flanagan, 1995, p. 63)

- 'Súil le cúiteamh a mhilleas an cearbhach' ('hope to recoup is what ruins the card player') or the equivalent expression 'súil le breis a mhileann an cearbhach' – the idea that some people mistakenly believe that the law of averages will mean that they can win back money that they have lost through gambling (Flanagan, 1995, p. 49)

27

Having considered the psychological significance of some Irish proverbs, let us now explain how they have been collected.

COLLECTION OF IRISH PROVERBS

A number of collections of Irish proverbs have been published in recent years (see Flanagan, 1995; MacCon Iomaire, 1999; Williams, 1992). One of the earliest of these collections is attributed to the legendary Cormac Mac Airt who is alleged to have compiled the 'Teagasc Chormaic' (Flanagan, 1995). Of published work, the three most important collections of Irish-language proverbs are *Seanfhocail na Mumhan* (published originally in 1926 but revised in 1984), *Sean-Fhocla Chonnacht* (published in two volumes in 1948 and 1952) and *Seanfhocail Uladh* (published originally in 1906 but revised in 1976). These three collections, together with proverbs found in the Schools' Collection Manuscripts (collected in the 1930s by the Irish Folklore Commission), are stored in the archives of the School of Irish, Celtic Studies, Irish Folklore and Linguistics at UCD Dublin.

The fact that we have several large collections of proverbs does not mean that any of our inherited sayings is distinctively Irish, however. Given our complex linguistic and cultural heritage, it is not really surprising that few of our proverbs were created in this country. Nevertheless, some expressions have been identified as being unique to our country – such as 'If the rowan tree is tall, even so it is bitter on the top' (Williams, 2003). By the way, Irish folklore about trees indicates that the rowan, or mountain ash, is associated with protective powers against evil – mainly because it possessed a bright flame of red berries (MacCoitir, 2003).

In general, Irish proverbs seem to be derived from two separate traditions – the Gaelic tradition (Irish language) and the Anglo-Irish tradition (English language). Of course, the claim that all proverbs, like oral folklore, are international goes back at least as far as MacAdam (1858) who suggested that 'are identical, or nearly so, in all countries, seeming, as it were, to be citizens of the world' (cited in Flanagan, 1995, p. 7). Interestingly, similarities have been observed between Irish proverbs and those found among other Celtic races (Gaffney and Cashman, 1974). For example, the Irish saying 'marriage at the dungheap and the Godparents far away' resembles 'marriage o'er the anvil, sponsorship o'er the sea' (Gaffney and Cashman, 1974, p. 8). There are also some parallels between Irish proverbs and those found in Jamaica. For example, the Irish saying 'he who lies with dogs rises with fleas' has a Jamaican equivalent 'when you sleep wid darg, you ketch him flea' (1974, p. 8).

PROVERBS AND THE NATIONAL CHARACTER

What can we infer about the Irish people and character from studying Irish proverbs? Here's one answer to such a question: 'I am convinced that we may learn, from the proverbs current among a people, what is nearest and dearest to their hearts, how honour and dishonour are distributed among them, what is of good, what of evil report in their eyes, with very much more which it can never be unprofitable to know'. This quotation appeared in the writing of Robert Shipboy MacAdam (see an account of his life in A. J. Hughes, 1998). MacAdam (1808–95) was a progressive Belfast industrialist who was passionate about the Irish language and a leading collector of Irish proverbs as well as songs and folklore. MacAdam recognised that the Irish language, although still very widely spoken during his life, was in the process of a very sharp decline. Therefore, he hoped to collect instances of proverbs before they disappeared: 'we, whose earliest years are associated with books and schools, cannot readily realize the condition of persons who have obtained all their education without them; and yet such is the case with the existing

Gaelic-speaking population of Ireland' (quoted in Hughes, 1998, p. 74). MacAdam foresaw that the coming of a national English language school system in Ireland would diminish the stock of important but unrecorded aspects of Irish language tradition, and on this basis sought to save as many aspects as possible for posterity. This was one rationale behind his manuscript, *Six Hundred Gaelic Proverbs Collected in Ulster*.

However, MacAdam also held to the idea that proverbs reveal something about the national character or psyche. Thus, in order to understand the 'native Irish population of Ulster', he felt it essential to collect and classify the proverbs they used. In his introduction to the *Six Hundred Proverbs*, for example, he makes the following point:

> The difference between the English and French people, for instance, could scarcely be better expressed than by two of their very familiar proverbs, both recommending courteous behaviour, but each for a reason peculiarly national:
>
> English: *Civility costs no money*
> French: *On attrape plus de mouches avec du miel qu'avec du vinaigre* ('one catches more flies with honey than with vinegar').
>
> The present collection may therefore serve to throw some light on the character of the native Irish population of Ulster (quoted in Hughes, 1998, p. 76).

See also the quotation from MacAdam at the beginning of chapter 8 in this book which makes the same point.

Such a perspective forms part of the rationale for this book also. The question is whether we can detect among popular Irish proverbs a distinct outlook and national mental framework. Was Francis Bacon correct when he speculated that proverbs serve as windows through which we can peer into the national character, 'The genius, wit and spirit of a nation are discovered in its proverbs' (Francis

Bacon, cited in MacCon Iomaire, 1999, p. vii)? This question is topical at present in view of the growing interest in Celtic culture and spirituality (Monaghan, 2001) as well as having a general validity. MacAdam's work is cited as a reminder that attempts to link character and culture are not novel. Nor is such a link accepted by all researchers in the area. In general, academic research on proverbs has taken one of two forms (Mieder and Holmes, 2000). On the one hand, some scholars have attempted to collect and classify proverbs under various headings in the absence of any particular theoretical approach. On the other hand, paremiologists have explored proverbs using the theories and methods of academic disciplines such as anthropology and psychology. Sometimes, these analyses have led to interesting if rather controversial conclusions on the relationship of character and proverbs. To illustrate, just as MacAdam noted the English and French capture the same phenomenon with different proverbs (see above), anthropologists have proposed that people of different nationalities may interpret the same proverb differently. For example, Milner (1971) claimed that English and Scottish people seem to differ in their interpretation of the proverb 'a rolling stone gathers no moss'. Specifically, whereas English people viewed this maxim in positive terms, their Scottish counterparts interpreted it negatively. The question as to whether the proverbs of a people 'contain in distilled form the essence of their philosophy of life and worldview' (Mieder and Dundes, 1981, p. 284) is not one that has been satisfactorily resolved and while folklorists have been wary of assuming that proverbs express national character, anthropologists are more likely to believe (like MacAdam) that proverbs collected from a people reflect their ideology.

Interestingly, the question was taken on specifically with regard to Ireland in a paper published in 1945 (and reprinted in Mieder and Dundes, 1981) by F. N. Robinson. He assessed a broad sample of proverbs then current in Ireland. On that basis and somewhat tentatively, he suggested one could find examples of 'local colour' as well as stylistic formulas in Irish proverbs. By the former, he was referring to local specificity with references to national historic or legendary figures as well as local customs. For example, the patron saint of Ireland, Patrick, made appearances in proverbs like, 'Ní ar aonchois tháinig Pátraic go hÉireann' ('Patrick did not come to Ireland on one leg', equivalent perhaps to the notion in English that a person should 'have more than one string to their bow'). The figure Etain also appears in proverbs such as, 'come cách co hEtain' ('Fair is every one until [compared with] Etain'). Specific Irish games and customs can appear in the expression noted earlier, 'is maith an t-iománaí an té a bhíonn ar an gclaí.'

Robinson also found evidence for specific stylistic Irish formulae which he called the 'deserves' or 'ought to' types (see Mieder and Dundes, 1981, p. 291) appearing with the Irish word, 'dligid', for example 'Dligid maith mórad' ('Good deserves to be magnified') or 'Dligid aide urraim' ('A teacher deserves respect'). The 'until' style (as used with the Etain proverb above) is also common; another example is 'Ugdhar gach neach go labhrann' ('Everyone is an authority until he speaks'). However, with regard to the broader question of whether proverbs represent national characters or traits, Robinson reports himself dubious. Robinson is particularly sceptical of the claim made by O'Muirgheasa, that Irish proverbs show great respect for women, a gallantry uniquely Irish. Robinson quotes a whole series of proverbs and triads where females are in fact disparaged very heavily ('Is fearr órlach gasúr no troigh cailín', 'Better is an inch of a boy than a foot of a woman'). This is not atypical: see also chapters 7 and 8 in this book for further examples. Robinson is willing to accept that there may be more frequent examples of such national traits as combativeness and humour in Irish proverbs but that other supposed characteristics such as piety and superstition are, if anything, understated. And the exhortation towards combat and bravery is common in Scandinavian folklore while humour is a common feature in virtually every country's proverbs, especially the use of exaggeration typical of Irish ones. Robinson concludes that his review has found very little evidence that 'national proverbs have been affected by their [Irish] character or temperament' (Mieder and Dundes, 1981, p. 296).

The issue of universality versus particularity (the idea that separate peoples may forge unique cultural paths) is a fundamental one to sociological reflections. The popular theory of 'modernisation' within social theory usually evokes a vague notion that as states develop, they go through industrialisation and become conscious nation states in the modern sense. The changes do not simply affect legal and political institutions; rather modernisation is taken to be 'a multi-faceted process involving changes in all areas of human thought and activity' (Huntingdon, 1968, p. 52). Does this imply that the proverbs of a country, as a consequence of social change, must inevitably lose their distinctiveness, or in the case of the distinctive proverbs, disappear from usage? But this seems to be an overly economistic interpretation of history. There is more, surely, to a society's development than industrialisation (although it probably is a key watershed, as a majority of the population go from working on the land to toiling in the cities, there are some predictable and virtually inevitable by-products – see below for a consideration of the importance of this change) and there are other factors at play. A powerful one is the experience of war and violence that a people may share, and perhaps that of oppression – as the oppressor, but especially psychologically important as the oppressed. The conquest of one country by another is of course not unique – in fact, to a large extent, that process, repeated hundreds and thousands of times *is* history – but the particular permutation of a Gaelic-speaking people being culturally dominated by an English one is. The consequences, even linguistically, are still being felt. For example, Dolan's (2004) *Dictionary of Hiberno-English* demonstrates that even if the Irish language was snuffed out in most parts of Ireland, it has forced its way back through English. As Dolan comments in introducing his

33

dictionary, 'Irish people use and speak English in a distinctive way. In vocabulary, construction, idiom, and pronunciation their speech is identifiable and marked . . . It is a macaronic dialect, a mixture of Irish and English, sometimes in the same word (e.g. 'girleen', 'maneen'). Hiberno-English has its own grammar, so obviously different in several ways from Standard English grammar that it may appear to be a "wrong grammar".' (2004: p. xxi). A classic example offered of this alternative grammar can be found in one use of the word, 'after' by Hiberno-English speakers. 'I'm after eating my dinner' as any Irish person recognises when another Hiberno-English speaker says it, means that 'I've recently eaten my dinner'. This reflects the Irish idiom, 'Tá mé tar éis mo dhinnéar a ithe'. Similarly, as we have shown above, the triadic form of proverb may well be Ireland's unique contribution to the structure of proverbs.

One must keep in mind that Irish folklore and proverbs were inevitably and fundamentally changed by the increasing presence and use of the English language, especially from the mid sixteenth century onwards. Although the same kinds of themes may emerge in Irish proverbs as in Scandinavia and continental Europe, their particular expression may be unique to each, because of the way language insists on evolving in discrete patterns. (And as Dolan points out, in Ireland, it was not merely a battle between Irish and English, since by the twelfth century there were four languages spoken on the island of Ireland: Irish; Latin by clerics and monks; Norman-French by the leaders of the invading Normans, and Early Middle English by their followers). And there are also claims to a specific Irish psyche and a method by which that psyche is expressed: 'The elision of the personal and the national, the way history becomes kind of a scaled-up biography, and biography a microcosmic history, is a particularly Irish phenomenon' (Foster, 2001, p. xi). The psyche may of course change, as Irish people suddenly become 'rich and well fed as never before' (Foster, 2001, p. xv) but its impact and intrusion into the language should remain visible for generations. In truth, the reader, not the authors, will have to decide whether a distinct Irish character exists *and* makes its presence known through the language(s) spoken in Ireland. Perhaps it does; or perhaps as Declan Kiberd has suggested, 'it may well be, however, that the very idea of Ireland – like the now deserted Great Blasket – is a kind of fiction which the mere islanders themselves are finding it harder and harder to sustain . . . All nations are, in Benedict Anderson's phrase, an invented or imagined community, and the Irish have shown more relish for that fiction than most' (Kiberd, 1989, p. 337).

PROVERBS AND CHANGE

An unintended or unplanned question that arose in assessing the nature of proverbs was the issue of social change and relevance of proverbs to an increasingly dynamic society. It was noted in chapter 1 that the highpoint of the proverb in European countries was the nineteenth century (in terms of usage) and since then it has gone into decline. It may be that proverbs operate optimally, in terms of providing useful folk wisdom on a topic, where there exists relative social and economic stability. This kind of stability is more likely to be associated with societies where agriculture dominates. Ideal habits and widespread knowledge and beliefs built on thousands of daily observations of the rhythms of lives in direct contact with the land can thus be enshrined in pithy, if occasionally contradictory aphorisms. However, it is clear that for the technologically advanced societies of Europe, the calm world of peasant agriculture gave way to the revolutionary dynamic of market relations and the hum of business in the late nineteenth century with a concomitant rise in urbanisation (and of course the process is not restricted to Europe: Hobsbawm (1994) has estimated that by around the end of the twentieth century, for the first time, a majority of the world's population no longer earned its livelihood directly from the land,

changing the pattern of several millennia). Inevitably, as a consequence of this change, older forms of knowledge are superseded,
forgotten or ignored and a greater premium is put on novelty, flexibility and openness to innovation rather than on socially crystallised
beliefs such as proverbs. Furthermore, where the populations are
increasingly likely to be literate – and the rise of mass education has
historically tended to accompany the other process like modern
capitalism and industrialisation – then less value is placed on orally
stored wisdom since books can be checked, records kept, almanacs
consulted and other information verified in similar ways.

Partly because of its troubled relationship with Britain as well as
for reasons of geography (peripheral to the huge economic engine
centred around Northern Italy, North Eastern France, Western
Germany, Belgium, Netherlands and South Eastern England) and,
it has been suggested, because of the psyche of its people, Ireland was
certainly not one of the early economically dynamic societies of
Europe. In fact, until the Lemass/Whitaker reforms of the 1950s, it
remained a stubbornly static or perhaps stagnant society. And it was
not until the 1990s that very sharp economic growth occurred along
with corresponding changes both in people's daily activities (the
rapid decline in those earning a living through agriculture) as well as
their beliefs (the erosion of traditional Catholicism). In a number of
chapters, we find ourselves running up against the reality of change
and querying whether proverbs born in a past committed to certainties
and stabilities can accommodate or fit to a present of obstinate,
dogmatic and self-conscious transformation. In chapters such as
those on the proverbs of interpersonal relationships as well as on food
and drink, the tension of change is discussed in further detail. Just as
with the question of the universality or particularity of Irish language,
the reader will have to decide whether proverbs actually represent
'timeless' wisdom or whether some or all have been rendered mere
historical curiosities.

STILL CHANGING: THE RISE OF ANTI-PROVERBS

So far in this chapter, we have seen that among the most interesting of proverbs are those which are dynamic and flexible expressions rather than fixed anachronisms. Inspired by this idea, some pare-miographers have deliberately developed 'anti-proverbs' or parodies of traditional figurative wisdom (Mieder, 2004). For example, the proverb 'A fool and his money are soon parted' has been transformed into such variants as 'A married man and his money are soon parted' or 'A widow and her money are soon courted'. Here, anti-proverbs follow the structure of the original expression while changing some of the words to reflect changing social assumptions or experiences. As Mieder (2004, p. 28) concluded, 'the fixity of proverbs is not as rigid as once was believed to be'. If this opinion is correct, then proverbs may evolve as much through humorous invention as through social influences. In this regard, it is instructive to consider how the expression 'A friend in need is a friend indeed' was parodied as 'A friend in weed (i.e., marijuana) is a friend indeed' during the drug-crazy 1970s in the US (Kirshenblatt-Gimblett, 1981).

To summarise, Irish people have long had great respect for folk traditions and expressions of traditional wisdom. This respect is deep-seated and ubiquitous. In this chapter, we have explored a number of issues arising from the role of proverbs in Irish society. We began by exploring the origin and characteristics of Irish proverbs and commenting on their psychological significance. After that, we examined the question of whether or not proverbs help us to understand certain aspects of 'Irishness'. Then, we sketched the relevance of proverbs in a changing Irish society. Finally, we touched on the rise of 'anti-proverbs'.

3

Food and Drink

'Síleann mo bholg go bhfuil mo scornach gearrtha'.
('My belly thinks my throat is cut', as the hungry man said.)

INTRODUCTION

In several of the other chapters, the historically contingent aspect of proverbs is stressed – in other words, that proverbs must fit the times or else go out of use. With food and drink (including alcohol), is it safe to assume that these are more-or-less constants, and that what once was the case regarding human nature in this domain continues to hold true? After all, what could be more straightforward than hunger? One expends energy, depletes calories and becomes hungry. The physiological basis of this is becoming understood: a region of the brain known as the hypothalamus can 'read' signals about nutrient-needs and fuel levels from signals in the blood. Some signals indicate hunger and others indicate satiety. However, the relationship between hunger and consumption is somewhat more complex than simply refuelling a car. Evidence has shown, for example, that people will eat more when foods have different flavours (a study carried out by the appropriately named Peck, 1978). Appetite is not always linked to hunger since even people who have eaten can be stimulated to eat more if presented with food that has a nice appearance or aroma. Our cultures are also very important in dictating both how much we eat (how frequently and how much should go on our plates) as well as the content. Bernstein et al. (2003), for example, note that many Mexicans pay a great deal to feast on delicacies such as baby alligators and insects while in Europe, most of us would pay *not* to eat such 'treats'. We shall see below that Irish society and its attitudes to food as well as consumption patterns have changed beyond recognition. This inevitably changes the context in which we should interpret proverbs. Alcohol, too, has changed its status and acceptability for the Irish population but perhaps less dramatically than food. Again, the physiological effects are constant – the impact of alcohol is due to the presence of ethanol, a substance with psychoactive properties with implications for human central nervous system functioning. Moderate to heavy amounts of alcohol reduce the ability of the brain to impose inhibitory control on the body generating memory loss, distortion in perception and slurring of speech. However, the loss of inhibition also creates a feeling of relaxation along with a short-term high, caused by alcohol's enhancement of endorphins, the body's natural painkillers.

These are the physiological processes behind the patterns of routine consumption of food and alcoholic drink. Food is inevitably a fundamental process of any human society; as we shall see, alcohol in Irish society has had an important historical role. However, cultural and historical factors have meant that the roles of both have changed. Studying proverbs about food and drink should provide us with both an informative view into the lives of the past as well as a sense about how far we have travelled from that past in relation to these fundamental aspects of everyday living.

DIET AND DRINK IN IRELAND:
THE HISTORICAL CONTEXT

We need to distinguish between a number of different ages in the history of Irish diet. The first is that of traditional Gaelic society which supported a system of 'semi-nomadic pastoral farming' (Connolly, 1998, p. 154) and where meat was eaten in relatively large quantities.

Milk and butter also played an important part in daily intake, with rancid butter on oatcakes being a popular dish. Cereals remained only a minor part of the diet though, until Anglo-Norman colonists introduced their use in gruels and puddings. Waves of English and Scottish colonisation from the sixteenth century onwards led to a further increase in tillage farming and the products of the sea (fish, oysters, cockles and mussels) came to be used more intensively as a source of food. The attitudes of the newcomers included their horror in the face of some aspects of Gaelic cuisine (for example, 'the consumption of blood, in a jellified form' or 'animal entrails . . . carrion and horse meat. . . [and] warm milk straight from the cow', Connolly, 1998, p. 155). Class distinctions in diet became sharper with the Irish gentry importing sugar, tea, coffee, raisins, currants and confectionary in increasing volume and having a diet that begins to look somewhat like our own, with meat, dairy products, cereals, and fruit becoming integrated. Disastrously (as it turned out), however, the poor peasantry became increasingly dependent on a New World import, the potato, which, per acre can generate a higher calorific output than cereals. Buttermilk was drunk with the potatoes and in the 'hungry months' of the summer, oatmeal and herrings 'filled the hiatus between the end of the old season's potato crop and the new harvest' (Connolly, 1998, p. 155). Following the Great Famine, food consumption even among the poor became more varied, thanks in part to the greater distribution of grocery products via the new train system.

The main alcoholic beverages to be consumed in medieval Ireland were ale and mead. Whiskey was used for medicinal purposes until probably the mid sixteenth century when it became popular as a drink in its own right. Again, class differences emerged: the gentry imported and consumed wine on a regular basis. The poor peasantry used alcohol but in a way that might be described as 'binge-drinking' in modern society, that is it was not part of their regular diet but was associated with special events of hospitality and celebration such as marriages, wakes, fairs, markets and religious festivals, when it was consumed very heavily. (See also chapter 6 for an extended discussion of the unusual nature of aspects of the Irish and so-called American 'wake'.) It was only with the gradual spread of illicit distillation technology that regular and frequent alcohol intake became the norm for many Irish rural-dwellers. By 1800, whiskey or an illicit home-distilled version of it was the most popular alcoholic drink in Ireland. (There are interesting echoes of this in the late John McGahern's acclaimed book, *That They May Face the Rising Sun*, where the setting is rural Ireland of the 1980s, but many of the habits such as the consumption of whiskey rather than beer or wine seem to link the characters to a more remote time in the past.) Heavy excise duty meant it became very difficult for small producers to continue, and in the early nineteenth century, today's prominent brand names such as Power's and Jameson's emerged from the consolidation of smaller whiskey houses. Excise duty not surprisingly led to greater production of 'poteen', a colourless spirit-alcohol produced by using barley or a similar cereal in the distillation process. The duty was bitterly resented and a prototype police force was used first against illicit distillers rather than land agitators (in 1817 in Donegal). The quality of poteen was, however, not always very reliable and this meant that commercially-produced, but more expensive whiskey remained attractive. 'Poteen' was considered to be a national Irish phenomenon but historical research now suggests that it was really only popular in the northern half of the country, reflecting the heavier reliance there on grain production rather than the dairy and cattle-fattening more typical of the south (see Connolly, 1998, p. 267).

In the post-famine era, a degree of urbanisation, the rise of the public house in town and village and the commercial growth of the Guinness brewery made pub life an accepted part of male culture in the country (not until the 1960s did female consumption of alcohol in public begin to lose its stigma). The Guinness brewery dynasty became one of the greatest successes in Ireland's commercial history: in 1759, Arthur Guinness moved his brewing concern from Leixlip into a disused brewery at St James's Gate near Dublin city centre. The company had expanded rapidly in the early nineteenth century when it branded and sold its porter beer as 'stout', 'extra stout' and 'triple stout'. In the post-famine period, it successfully penetrated the British market (and was registered as one of the top ten largest companies in the world by the 1930s).

THE MODERN ERA

In the modern era, consumption in Ireland has expressed itself in qualitatively different ways from in the past. While the latter half of the twentieth century did not witness any widespread hunger or serious nutritional deprivation in Ireland, most observers and indeed citizens now regard the bulk of that era as one in which there was a certain grim 'survivalism' in Irish eating patterns. Drab eating patterns and infrequent but heavy alcohol consumption were the rule. In the last decade of that century, though, the patterns altered radically: crude quantitative statistics reveal that per capita consumption of every foodstuff remorselessly and steadily increased in a year-on-year pattern. This reflected the 'Celtic Tiger' era, as the Irish economy, much to everyone's surprise it should be noted, became remarkably buoyant. The consistent GDP growth 'fed' into a consumption mentality, in a metaphorical but also literal way. Outside observers had once commented on the parochialism of Irish cuisine, and its limits, as well as, *inter alia*, the trials of finding balsamic vinegar anywhere in the land. But in the 1990s, all that changed. It was not just Dublin that revelled in new cosmopolitan tastes but even small rural towns that now wouldn't be seen dead without their lunchtime panini and take-away lemongrass-seasoned Thai dishes. The consequences, aside presumably from educating a

43

whole generation of callow tastebuds to new heights of refinement, were remarkably similar to those noted by the economist and
commentator J. K. Galbraith, in his celebrated book, *The Affluent
Society*. In that book, he considered the effects of economic growth
on the US population from the 1950s and commented that: 'more die
in the United States of too much food than of too little. Where the
population was once thought to press on the food supply, now . . .
the food supply presses on the population' (Galbraith, 1969, p. 118).
This serves as a neat description of the contrasts of contemporary
Ireland: while an older generation can recall pre-Second World
War and wartime privations and their attendant health problems,
in the modern era adult but especially childhood obesity and dia-
betes through over-consumption of sugary goods have become the
targets of contemporary concern. As we write, the Department of
Health and Children and the Health Promotion Unit-backed
conference, 'Tackling Obesity Together' has just concluded, its
main concern being the rocketing dietary problems associated with
over-consumption. The Department of Health and Children has
also put alcohol consumption firmly in its sights as a serious problem in Ireland and estimated that the financial cost of the health
problems associated with it in 2003 was over €2.65 billion. Irish
alcohol consumption per capita is now the second highest of the
25 EU countries and the rate of increase in consumption has been
the fastest in Europe. But the change in alcohol consumption has
been qualitative, as well as quantitative. The pattern until the 1990s
was of overwhelming reliance on the staples of beer and spirits
(especially stouts, lagers and whiskies). In the recent past, though,
wine consumption has become popular, with meals, but also on its
own and wine pages are now a fixed item in virtually every weekend
newspaper. The ban on smoking in public places (including public
houses) seems likely to continue a momentum towards forms of
alcohol consumption outside the traditional pub venue.

44

Where the context has changed so remarkably in a relatively short amount of time, one must assume it is at least possible that proverbs can no longer offer insight into a society that is 'changed utterly'. On the other hand, some may believe that proverbs provide a lasting comment on the society from which they spring and are relatively resistant to short-term trend swings. We shall evaluate these competing possibilities below. With regard to food and drink consumption, the central question becomes: is there an underlying style or consistency to consumption patterns in Ireland that remains constant despite surface changes? Certainly, if we follow the traditional distinction between manifest (or outward appearance) and latent (or core expression at a profound or foundation level), then there is no argument at the manifest or surface level: Irish society has undergone a remarkable 'foodie' revolution. The only doubt remains over the latent underlying *style* of consumption.

THEMES IN FOOD AND DRINK PROVERBS

A surprising thing about food-related proverbs is the considerable number that are not really about food at all, but simply use its consumption as a metaphor for something else. A very common form contrasts someone who is enthusiastic at dining but shirks hard work. Examples include, 'First at the pot and last at the work', or similarly, 'A man at the food and a weakling at the work' (both from Gaffney and Cashman, 1974, p. 42). O'Farrell (1980) provides us with 'A man at the food should be a man at the work', p. 42, while Williams (1992, p. 16), 'Fear ag an bhia is dearóil san obair' ('The worst at work is first at the table'), and similarly, 'Tús ag an phota is deireadh ag an obair' ('Last to the work, first to the table'). And from the Irish Proverbs collection on CD (Fios Feasa, 1998) comes the wry observation, 'An cóngar chun an bhídh is an timpeall chun na hoibre' ('The shortcut to food and the long way around to work'). A

45

slightly more poetic turn of phrase is offered in 'Eat yourself into a doaghy dandily and you'll dwine' and O'Farrell (1980, p. 42) interprets this as, 'Eat yourself into an inactive, overindulgent youth and you'll ail slowly'. We can see, though, that the strong theme coming through these proverbs is that a large appetite must be justified by the muscle power expended in labour. A society heavily dependent on largely non-mechanised agriculture could demand no less.

Other proverbs that mention food but are really about personality are the character-revealing ones. These can be found in 'A blunt knife shows a bad housekeeper' and 'As is the cook, so is the kitchen' (from Williams, 1992, p. 16). Obviously the assumption here is that our traits are best revealed in everyday routine activity. Aside from these proverbs about character, there is also a nice reflection on satiety and its effects, in the proverb, 'Cha dtuigeann bró sháitheach bró thámhach' ('A full stomach never thinks of an empty one'). This may mean either that it is difficult for those who are satiated to feel a sense of empathy for those who are hungry, or (and more subtly), when a person is sated, it is difficult to imagine being hungry, or even indeed to think about food.

Finally, in this 'not-really-about-food' category, there are proverbs that appear to be straightforwardly about food but must be as much about people (just as 'don't judge a book by its cover' is rarely used literally about books). O'Farrell (1980, p. 41) cites examples such as, 'the crab tree has a sweet blossom', the implication being that pretty facades can disguise sourness underneath. Or, alternatively, 'it takes a lot of hard work to turn a bitter damson into a sweet jelly' is a perhaps less colourful than 'you can't make a silk purse from a sow's ear'. Presumably, the advice that it is worth looking beyond or below the surface is intended to be inferred from, 'There are more knobs in the buttermilk than what you see floating', from O'Farrell (1980, p. 42) or 'The first drop of the soup is hottest but the most wholesome lies below' (p. 43). In a similar vein, Williams (1992, p. 16) lists, 'You don't know what is in the pot till the lid is lifted'. A warning to people not to forget their often humble origins comes from the expression 'some people, when they get their heads above the churn would not drink buttermilk' (Williams, 1992, p. 18). It seems probable that many of these types of proverbs began as direct observations and were then picked up and used in other contexts to aid people in driving home their points.

A second broad theme is one we will meet again in chapter 5, proverbs about money; the specific theme is one of straightforward advice. Where literacy could not be taken for granted and the use of written recipes was undoubtedly rare, such down-to-earth rules would have been far from patronising for those involved in preparing food. 'The juice of the cow alive or dead is good' is provided by Gaffney and Cashman (1974, p. 42), outlining both advice as well as revealing the ways in which calories (through milk or blood) were obtained from livestock. In Williams (1992, p. 18) and also O'Farrell (1980, p. 42), there are a number of versions offered of the Gaelic phrase, 'Maistreadh fada a níos an drochim' ('long churning makes bad butter' or 'the longer the churning the tougher the butter'), practical advice in a time, as Williams points out, before creameries were widespread and thus each house had to churn its own butter as practically a daily activity. A different form of guidance is found in, 'Taste the food and you'll get a taste for it'; this is remarkably modern in the context of helping children overcome their nervousness for new foods, since many experts advise the 'one taste rule', that is that children should be asked to taste at least a mouthful of novel foods rather than rejecting them out of hand. Further suggestions, chiming with modern recommendations about nutrition can be found in, 'He sups ill, who eats all at dinner', since regular moderate portions are usually preferred now, from a health point of view, to the model of a long abstention followed by a very heavy meal. Further domestic pointers can be found in proverbs like, 'a good fire makes a speedy cook' (Williams, 1992, p. 16 – Ní tine mhaith cócaire tapaidh – this could obviously be broadened to mean more generally that those who prepare well will enjoy easier success), 'Cool before you sup' (Williams, 1992, p. 17 – Fuaraigh sula n-óla tú – this too can be extended to general situations where one should look before one leaps, or let one's ardour cool before one chooses), or in the following suggestion that small amounts of food or tasters can be pleasing, 'A little tastes sweet' (Williams, 1992, p. 17 – Bíonn blas ar an bheagán), with its nod towards the 1970s revolution in nouvelle cuisine and quality above quantity. In contrast to this rather precious adage though is the more robust, 'What won't choke will fatten and clean dirt is no poison' (Williams, 1992, p. 16). In other words, don't be too squeamish at the dinner table. One proverb that is cited by both Gaffney and Cashman (1974, p. 42) and Williams (1992, p. 16) is 'Help is always welcome except at the table' (Is maith an rúd cúnamh, ach ag an mbord). The threat of too many cooks may be intended here – although it may also refer to displeasure in having to share food – and indeed social psychological research into group versus individual productivity suggests that often the individual effort is to be preferred over the group one (since in the latter situation, everyone claims credit but their input is harder to measure). Control and direction of the kitchen also almost certainly reflected the holding of power in the domestic domain and having counterclaims of authority would have contributed to discordance.

A surprising theme, albeit a somewhat rare one, is the sensual pleasure provided by food. In a society where explicit eroticism was taboo, the delight of food is sometimes implied as a sexual one. A fairly innocent version is provided by, 'kissing is as sweet as good cooking but it doesn't satisfy as long' (O'Farrell, 1980, p. 41). A more ambiguous one is also cited in O'Farrell (1980, p. 42), 'It's a good wife whose mouth is your mirror', in relation to food, it is suggested. But there are more explicit proverbs where the wife's duty is to keep her husband content in the kitchen and the bedroom: 'Feed him the finest brown bread and he'll stay, but feed him on clokes and forever he'll stray' or very robustly, 'Any army may march on its stomach but

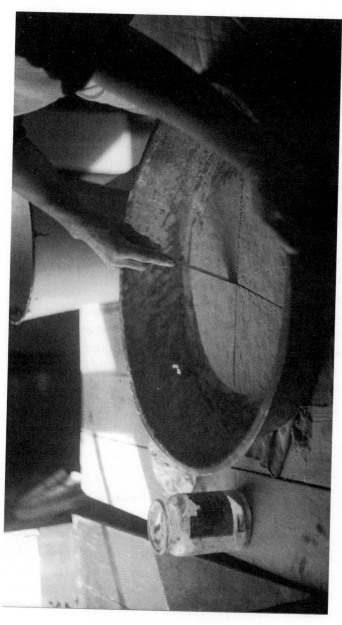

Feed him the finest brown bread and he'll stay, but feed him on clokes and forever he'll stray.
Making bread, Dun Chaoin, County Kerry (1947).

a husband always makes love on it' (both from O'Farrell, 1980, p. 42). The converse, the possibility of food introducing, or perpetuating, strife in/to a relationship is made clear in the proverb, 'Eaten bread is soon forgotten – except when it's baked by a complaining wife' (O'Farrell, 1980, p. 43). The recommendation against adultery can be found running though 'Don't scald your lips with another man's porridge' (Williams, 1992, p. 20). Even warnings against same-sex activity can be found, as in 'Champ [mashed potato] to champ will choke you' or 'Butter to butter is no kitchen' (Im le him chan tarsann é), used, Williams suggests (1992, p. 19), when two men or two women were seen either dancing or kissing. Less tantalisingly, though, these proverbs may be simply recommending a varied diet!

The awesome power of food to frustrate, sicken or control also emerges from several other proverbs. 'It's dear bought butter that's licked off a briar', or more literally, 'he who is fond of nettle honey pays too dear for it' ('An té arb ansa leis mil as neantóig, íocann sé ródhaor'; Williams, 1992, p. 19) is a nice, if strange image of the frustrations of hunger. 'A fast cook causes a faster pain' (O'Farrell, 1980, p. 41) highlights the danger of food. Matching the food to the correct time of day can also be found in O'Farrell (p. 42), 'food is gold in the morning, silver in the afternoon but lead at night'. The power of food or rather its absence, hunger, to motivate is also made clear: 'hunger will conquer a lion' or 'hunger is a good sauce, if it doesn't choke you, it will fatten you' (both from Williams, 1992, p. 15).

ALCOHOL (THE DEMON)

There are relatively few warnings about the dangers of food, only its absence or poor-preparation. (And indeed why would there be? It is so very recently that over-consumption has become a serious health issue.) On the other hand, the proverbs connected with alcohol are almost entirely one sided: they present in totality a long note of alarm about the perils of imbibing. One searches almost in vain to find something positive about the noble rot. Even the three proverbs that appear to promote alcohol do so in a wry way, hinting more of desperation: 'A man in need of a drink thinks of wider schemes than the great generals of our time' and 'morning is the time to pity the sober. The way they're feeling is the best they're going to feel all day' (both from O'Farrell, 1980, p. 31) – these have a jauntier feel than other proverbs and may have been collected as observed in usage in pubs etc. rather than from the literature). There is also an ambiguity about 'The cure of the drinking is to drink again' (from Gaffney and Cashman, 1974, p. 36), interpretable as either a reckless hair-of-the-dog abandonment, or alternatively a warning about the addictive aspects of drink. One can be assured that the negative bias towards alcohol was not a direct reflection of social behaviour – that everybody detested and eschewed grape and grain. Undoubtedly it was the converse: the powerful magnet of intoxication and disinhibition in a society, where pleasures were rare and worries grave and ceaseless, shaped a strong ideological message against alcohol, reflected in widely used phrases. A powerful threat was obviously the poverty and ruin associated with expending very scarce resources on alcohol: 'The drunkard will soon have daylight in through the rafters' (An té a leanas ól, chan fada go dtiocfaidh solas an lae isteach ar mhullach an toighe). Or also from Williams (1992, p. 24), a proverb that sums up the squalor of the drunk: 'The three faults of drink is [sic]: a sorrowful morning, a dirty coat, and an empty pocket' (Trí bhua an ólacháin: maidin bhrónach, cóta salach, pócaí folamha). The ruinous nature of alcoholism is laid out in the starkest of proverbs: 'A man takes a drink; the drink takes a drink; the drink takes the man' (O'Farrell, 1980, p. 30). 'Wine drowns more men than water' and 'wine is sweet but the results are bitter' (from Williams, 1992, p. 23), 'There's little profit in constant drunkenness' (O'Farrell, 1980, p. 31). What could be more direct than, 'Thirst is a shameless disease'? Financial devastation is highlighted: 'sweet is the wine but sour is the payment' and 'it's sweet to drink but bitter to pay for it'. Or more poetically, 'Thirst after the drink and sorrow after the money' (Gaffney and Cashman, 1974, p. 36). Nationalism is subtly played upon in one proverb to drive the point home: 'The devil invented Scotch [whisky] to make the Irish poor' (O'Farrell, 1980, p. 31). Or a certain class resentment is stoked in another proverb, 'You've never seen a flagday for a needy publican' (O'Farrell, 1980, p. 30), suggesting that boozing is essentially a mug's game, playing into the hands of the publican.

Other proverbs highlight the *loss of control* associated with alcohol. From O'Farrell, we find the following examples of this: 'Practice makes perfect, there's many do think, But a man's not too perfect when he's practised at drink' (1980, p. 30) as well as 'Before you call for one for the road, be sure you know the road' (1980, p. 30). Similarly, Gaffney and Cashman include in their collection, 'You take your health once too often to the whiskey shop till it gets broken' (p. 35). Perhaps even more shaming were the *psychological* aspects of alcoholism, the dependence, addiction and obsession. These are nicely captured in the image of 'He'll never comb a grey hair because of his drinking' and even more simply, 'Thirst begets greater thirst' (O'Farrell, 1980, p. 31), or 'The end of drinking is more thirst' (Gaffney and Cashman, 1974, p. 35). The restless desire for alcohol is described, with some colour, in proverbs such as, 'He'd step over ten naked women to get at a pint' (O'Farrell, 1980, p. 30) or, on the same theme, 'If Holy Water was porter, he'd be at mass every morning' (O'Farrell, 1980, p. 31; in Gaffney and Cashman (1974, p. 35), 'whiskey' is substituted for 'porter'). A well-known aspect of alcohol's impact on the psychology of its user is the aggression that comes over otherwise mild-mannered individuals. This does not escape the notice of the proverb-makers either: 'It [whiskey] would make a rabbit spit at a dog' (Gaffney and Cashman, 1974, p. 35), or, with yet more feeling, 'Drink is the curse of the land. It makes you fight with your neighbour. It makes you shoot at your landlord – and it makes you miss him' (O'Farrell, 1980, p. 30).

The reader may have observed how many of the proverbs seem to assume or imply that the drinker is male. Drinking was almost certainly a disproportionately male activity in the past, but there are a few proverbs indicating both that at least some women drank, but also the greater shame accruing to them, 'A drunken woman is lost to shame', 'It is only folly to treat an old woman to a dram' (both from Gaffney and Cashman, 1974, p. 35). It is not too implausible to think that alcohol's short-term inhibiting effects helped men to, at least temporarily, overcome their inhibitions in communicating with one another. It would be straining the argument a little to think that this was their principal aim in consuming whiskey or beer, and in fact the available proverbs largely indicate that more open communication was a problem rather than a bonus. 'Drunkenness will not protect a secret' and 'Wine reveals the truth' are in Gaffney and Cashman's collection of proverbs (1974, p. 35) while Williams (1992, p. 24) has the more cryptic, 'empty kettles never leak'. And with a little more affection, O'Farrell has, 'A drink is shorter than a good yarn about it', and 'the truth comes out when the spirit comes in' (1980, pp. 30, 31).

Overall, what can we conclude in reflecting on the proverbs dealing with alcohol? The tone, as noted, is very largely a negative one, threatening the user with loss of control, ruin, being suckered by the publican, or (worse!) the British. The obsessive, addictive character of alcoholism is highlighted as is its frequent connection to aggressive behaviour. Men turn into blabbermouths after too much of the stuff, and women are even more lost to decency. And yet, it is clear from the historical records that Ireland has never been, nor entertained being, a state where alcohol was prohibited. Indeed as Tom Hayden (2001) has noted, among Catholic Irish-Americans heavy drinking was seen by many as a way of expressing their Irishness and link to the Old Country. (This phenomenon is referred to by member of Alcoholics Anonymous as 'CIA' – Catholic Irish Alcoholism.) At least a substantial minority of the population consumed a good deal of alcohol throughout the last few centuries, and

53

must have derived some enjoyment from it, despite the damage wrought on the lives of a small section of users. So why do we not find any trace of the positive in these proverbs? Why is alcohol given the role of the villain so consistently? If, as the psychologists Morgan and Grube (1994) have pointed out, Ireland has historically had an *ambivalent*, rather than an entirely *negative* attitude towards alcohol, why do proverbs take on the tone so entirely of the latter?

It may be that proverbs played an advisory role in society – creating awareness in a time when public health campaigns were unknown. Ireland as a wealthy modern society has tremendous problems with alcohol abuse; for a poorer society, where there was little or no surplus for luxuries or fripperies, survival meant warning as many as possible off regular alcohol consumption. (It is not surprising then that consumption occurred via binge drinking during life-milestone events such as weddings and wakes.) Proverbs transmitted the concerns about alcohol and its potential for ruin to those who were converted (teetotallers) and non-converted (drinkers) alike, hoping to help the former continue to abstain, and the latter to reduce the intake as much as possible. Thus in this light, the pro- verbs may be seen as a form of social evolution, arising in response to a new threat to social stability. Indeed, it is interesting to reflect on the passage of time required for a society to develop these kinds of defences. The peoples of the eastern Mediterranean and Mesopotamia were the first to develop alcohol through the production of wine. Today, it is common for Irish tourists on holidays to reflect on the sensible use of alcohol one tends to see among Italians and Greeks for example as well as the virtual non-usage among the Arab nations, although some of them, such as the Lebanese, do export wine. Presumably this wariness and caution towards alcohol took centuries of social experience and attitudinal experience to arise. As we move towards European nations which have come to alcohol later, we find far greater problems today with alcohol usage. The French, for example, were introduced to wine by the Romans and Holland

(2003) reports that the Romans were forbidden, on pain of death, from selling vines to the Gauls so that they became dependent on the Romans instead for the finished product. (The exchange rate was one large vase of wine in return for one slave and the Gauls' attempts at unity were thwarted by their continuous inter-tribal raiding to obtain slaves). The pattern of consumption for the Gaul novices was to drink the wine very strong, unlike the Romans who diluted it with water, and to take it in quickly until they collapsed (see Holland, 2003). Similarly, British sailors in the sixteenth and seventeenth centuries were notorious for the speed at which they could become drunk by simply downing rum directly for three to four minutes. Again, widespread alcohol use would have spread from France to the UK via the importation of claret from Bordeaux. And while western European societies continue to 'learn' how to deal with alcohol, it is clear that for still newer recruits to alcohol such as the Aboriginal peoples of Australasia, and the native Americans and Innuit of Northern America, the relatively recent introduction of alcohol to their communities and societies can also be seen to have disastrous consequences for many of their members. For example, in Thomas Keneally's book, *The Chant of Jimmie Blacksmith* (1972), the eponymous [anti-]hero is shocked to see the revered tribal chief and priest incoherently drunk on cooking sherry and begging passing whites for more. It seems likely that one way in which societies evolve to deal with new threats and to benefit from the lived experience of others is through common stores of oral knowledge such as in proverbs. Hence the bulk of the Irish proverbs' expression of hostility to alcohol-usage is a reflection of a society learning to deal with a seductive, powerful but potentially ruinous new challenge.

4

Weather Lore: Signs and Proverbs

'Ní hé lá na báistí lá na bpáistí'
('The day of rain is not the day of children')

INTRODUCTION

Anyone who has ever tried to entertain young children when it is too wet to go outside – especially on holidays – will surely appreciate the accuracy of the proverb above. After all, there is nothing quite like relentless Irish rain to achieve the twin feats of dampening people's spirits and increasing their irritability. Clearly, our 'weather', or the atmospheric conditions that prevail at any given time or place, provides a familiar if somewhat mysterious backdrop to our daily lives. This backdrop can be literal, as in the case of minding children on a rainy day, or metaphorical, as when people speak of being 'under the weather', when they feel unwell or of 'making heavy weather' of a task when it proves to be unexpectedly difficult. In this latter context, the misery of working in inclement weather has long been recognised in Irish folk wisdom. For example, an old saying warns us of 'The four worst things: ploughing in frost, harrowing in rain, making a ditch in summer and building a wall in winter' (Williams, 1992). Nevertheless, climatic adversity has inspired many Irish writers. The damp tapestry of Frank McCourt's early life is evoked in *Angela's Ashes* by a vivid account of how 'great sheets of rain gathered to drift slowly up the River Shannon and settle forever in Limerick', thereby creating 'a cacophony of hacking coughs, bronchial rattles, asthmatic wheezes, consumptive croaks' (McCourt, 1996, p. 1). Similarly, John McGahern (2002, p. 149), in *That They*

May Face the Rising Sun, portrays the soggy atmosphere of a rural Irish landscape by revealing how 'the air was so heavy it was like breathing rain'. Incidentally, it is notable that certain Irish weather phrases are surprisingly poetic and rich in imagery. For example, a cold morning has been described as one which causes people to 'kiss the knee-caps' ('ag pógadh na gcopán') – or to curl up in bed with their knees underneath their chins. Drawing upon this rich linguistic tradition, the purpose of the present chapter is to explore Irish weather wisdom distilled from various traditional prognostic sayings and proverbs.

In order to achieve this purpose, the chapter is organised as follows. To begin with, we shall comment briefly on the enduring appeal of Irish weather as a conversation piece. After that, we shall provide a brief overview of the Irish climate and consider some folk memories associated with it. Next, we shall examine the nature and validity of selected weather observations and prognostic signs. Finally, we shall explore some key Irish weather proverbs and their significance.

THE APPEAL OF IRISH WEATHER

Modifying Dr Johnson's famous remark in *The Idler* (1758), it seems that when two Irish people meet, their first conversation is usually about the weather. Why are we so preoccupied with climatic conditions in Ireland? The obvious reason is that Irish weather is quite capricious and unpredictable – and that this uncertainty raises a host of different conversational angles and possibilities between people. Supporting this view, an Irish phrase describes the multitude of different weather conditions that one can encounter in this country on any given day: 'Lá na seacht síon – gaoth mhór, báisteach, sioc agus sneachta, tintreach, toirneach agus lonrú gréine' ('On the day of seven weathers, there is high wind, frost and snow, thunder, lightning and sunshine'). Clearly, such phrases support the adage that if one does not like the weather in this country, all one has to do is wait a moment for it to change! And yet, some people are never happy with the weather – even when it is exceptionally pleasant. For example, consider the Irish saying that 'Dá mbeadh soineann go Samhain, bheadh breall ar dhuine éigin' ('If fine weather lasted until November, somebody would be pouting'). This proverb captures the idea that one cannot please everyone all the time. But what else can we learn from folk sayings about our prevailing climate? Before addressing this question, we need to learn a little more about the Irish climate.

THE IRISH CLIMATE

Because of its location above the equator on the north-western edge of Europe, the island of Ireland has a temperate climate which is characterised by rainfall throughout the year coupled with relatively small variation in temperature. The prevailing winds are warm (because they pass over the warm current known as the North Atlantic Drift) and westerly and blow in mainly from the Atlantic ocean. In general, these winds tend to reduce the heat of summer but also lessen the cold of winter. For this reason, the Irish climate has gained some surprising admirers over the years. For example, McWilliams (1999, p. 119) quotes Austin Bourke (a former Director of the Irish Meteorological Service) in a euology to our climate as follows: 'If each country in the world could temporarily detach itself from its climate, and if the various climates were placed on show in a public place, then we Irish would be trampled underfoot in the headlong rush of those who wished to take ours in place of theirs'!

In spite of this hyperbole about our climate, there are at least two natural catastrophes of the nineteenth century which were so powerful that they instantly entered Irish folk-memories. These

events were 'oíche na gaoithe móire' ('the night of the big wind') in
the late 1830s and the Great Famine between 1845 and 1850.
Although precise details of the causes and consequences of these
disasters lie beyond the scope of this chapter, the ways in which they
were explained at the time are interesting psychologically. By way of
background, on the night of the 'big wind' (Sunday 6 January 1839),
an intense storm (or perhaps a hurricane) that had been caused by a
deep depression over the Atlantic swept eastwards across the country.
It demolished buildings, destroyed forests and livestock and led
directly to about one hundred deaths (see Carr, 1991). Perhaps not
surprisingly, in view of its scale and sudden onset, this storm stimulated much popular folklore and several supernatural explanations
(McWilliams, 1999). For example, some people thought that the
storm had been a warning from God that the end of the world was at
hand. This explanation stemmed from the fact that the storm had
occurred on the feast of the Epiphany (which celebrates the coming
of the Magi) as well as from the belief that 7 January would be the
Day of Judgement. Others attributed the 'big wind' to the influence
of the fairies. This theory arose from the fact that 5 January coincided
with the feast of St Ceara – a night on which the 'little folk' were
believed to hold their celebrations and revelry. But the night of the
big wind is also significant in Irish cultural history for another
reason. Briefly, when the 'old age pension' scheme was introduced
in 1909, it entitled people aged over seventy years to avail themselves
of a small weekly allowance. But as many old people lacked docu-
mentary proof of their ages at that time because of the inaccuracy and
unreliability of birth registration records, the Government introduced an imaginative verification scheme whereby it granted this
pension to those who could 'prove' their age by providing a vivid
personal recollection of the night of the big wind (Akenson, 2005).

Climatic factors are also implicated in the second natural disaster
of nineteenth-century Ireland, namely, the Great Famine. This
disaster led to a million deaths in, and chronic emigration from, the

country. The potato blight which caused this famine was spread mainly by a combination of high temperatures and great humidity. When this blight spread across the country, it ravaged crops and destroyed the main source of nutrition of the vast majority of Irish people at that time. As in the case of the 'big wind', in the search for explanations of the famine, ominous portents such as eclipses of the sun in 1842 and in 1846 in Ireland attracted great popular attention at that time (Ó hÓgáin, 2002).

Having addressed the issue of folk memory of climatic events in Ireland, let us now examine some 'weather lore' – understood here as traditional beliefs about, comments on and/or predictions concerning weather conditions.

WEATHER OBSERVATIONS, SIGNS AND SUPERSTITIONS

In the interests of economic survival, people (especially, farmers, sailors and shepherds) have tried to anticipate impending weather conditions through careful observation of a variety of natural phenomena. Indeed, long before the advent of scientific weather forecasting, changes in the position of the sun, moon, stars, clouds and waves were studied for prognostic purposes. The folk expressions encapsulating these natural observations have been variously called 'predictive sayings', 'weather rules' and 'weather signs' (Mieder, 2004). Sometimes, this weather lore is expressed in rhymes. Consider 'When squirrels early start to hoard, winter will pierce us like a sword' (Simons, 2005a, p. 71). The prediction here is that when squirrels collect large supplies of nuts to hoard, a cold winter is likely to occur. Another weather rhyme is the familiar saying 'red sky at night, shepherd's delight; red sky in the morning, shepherd's warning' – an expression which dates back to biblical times. For example, in Matthew 16: 2–3, Jesus said to the fishermen 'When it is evening, ye say, "It will be fair weather: for the sky is red", and in the morning, "It will be stormy today for the sky is red ad threatening"'. This observation about the weather is echoed in several Irish phrases concerning the significance of red skies (McWilliams, 1999):

> Dearg anuas, fearthainn is fuacht;
> Dearg anoir, fearthainn is sioc;
> Dearg aníos, fearthainn is gaoth;
> Dearg aniar, tuineadh is grian

> Red high up, rain and cold;
> Red in the east, rain and ice;
> Red low down, rain and wind;
> Red in the west, fine weather and sunshine

Interestingly, modern meteorology supports the 'red sky at night . . .' rhyme (McWilliams, 1994). Briefly, the colour that we see in the sky is the result of the obstruction or scattering of sunlight by dust particles in the atmosphere. These particles distort the shorter wavelengths in the colour spectrum (blue, indigo and violet) more than the longer ones (orange and red). And so, a red sky at night is caused by sunlight passing through dust particles in the air to the west, where the sun sets. As dust usually indicates dry weather, and since in the northern hemisphere, weather fronts tend to approach from the west, a red sky at night tends to indicate that that a rain-front has just passed and that high-pressure weather is approaching. By contrast, a red sky in the morning in the eastern sky indicates that a dry weather front has probably passed already from west to east – suggesting that some low-pressure, wet or stormy weather is imminent. However, this explanation is controversial.

Historically, certain kinds of weather activity, such as eclipses of the sun or moon, have been interpreted as portents of impending disaster or as some form of punishment by angry gods. In Greek and Roman mythology, thunder and lightning had a special significance.

Among the ancient Greeks, a lightning flash indicated the displeasure of Zeus. For the Romans, lightning flashing from left to right across the sky was usually regarded as a harbinger of good weather. However, if it appeared to go in the opposite direction, the gods were thought to be angry and misfortune was likely.

As in many other mythologies around the world, the sun and moon were significant omens for the ancient Irish. Indeed, people worshipped and swore by these planets in pagan Ireland – as is evident in such expressions as 'dar brí na gréine is na gealaí' ('by the strength of the sun and the moon') (see Ó hÓgáin, 2002). In the pre-Christian era, the sun was portrayed as a god of the heavens which 'lay down' in the evening. Perceived in this way, the sun's long rays were interpreted as its 'legs' (Ó hÓgáin, 2002). Furthermore, certain weather signs could be detected from the position of these legs. In particular, thin, straggling legs were regarded as omens of bad weather: 'An ghriain agus cosa fúithi – drochshíon'. Conversely, when the sun's legs appeared to be up in the morning and down in the evening, good weather was believed to be imminent: 'Togha na hamisire chugainn – cosa na gréine suas ar maidin agus síos tráthnóna' (Rosenstock, 2000). Other bodies like the moon were also thought to presage certain kinds of weather conditions. For example, bad weather was likely if the moon appeared to be 'sitting down' in the sky: 'Leathghealach ghiortach ar a tóin – drochshíon'. By the way, the saying that 'The moon of the stubble-fields is the brightest of the year' (or 'Gealach na gcoinleach is gile sa bhliain'; Partridge, 1978) reflects a shrewd observation that the harvest moon (the September full moon or the one that occurs close in time to the Autumn Equinox; McWilliams, 2005b) appears to be unusually large and bright. A similar phenomenon occurs around mid-October and is known as the hunter's moon; McWilliams, 2005b). Despite the compelling impression of the moon's exaggerated size on these occasions, however, the experience is illusory. To explain, it is widely known in psychology that a full moon appears to be larger when it is near the horizon than when it is high in the sky. This 'moon illusion' can be overcome quite simply with the aid of a coin. Briefly, if one holds out a coin at arm's length so that it appears to cover the moon, it does not matter whether the moon is low down or high up because the image of the moon on one's retina remains the same regardless of its location. The most plausible explanation for this illusion is that when the moon is near the horizon, there are several cues to suggest that it is actually very far away.

Just as they explored the movements of the planets as harbingers of certain climatic conditions, our ancestors also investigated weather signs yielded by the behaviour and reproductive cycles of flora and fauna. For example, a great deal of weather lore developed from observations of the time that trees came into leaf. Thus the English rhyme 'oak before the ash, we shall have a splash; ash before oak, we shall have a soak' may seem to ring true. Invariably, such prognostic signs became enshrined in popular folklore and pro-verbial wisdom that was subsequently passed from one generation to another. However, perhaps not surprisingly, much of this lore is rooted more in superstition than in science. Consider the peculiar meteorological phenomenon when rain falls while the sun is shining. This unusual situation is interpreted superstitiously in almost every folklore tradition of the world. Among the events that it allegedly signifies are the devil 'getting married' (Bulgarian), the devil 'beating his wife' (Hungarian) or that 'the gypsies are washing their children' (Finnish) (Mieder, 2004). Another interesting weather superstition stems from the common belief that certain animals have an instinctive sensitivity to weather changes. It has been suggested that when a cat washes behind its ears, rain is on the way (Roud, 2003). An Irish version of this traditional weather sign is the saying that 'Sneachta chugainn nuair a níonn an cat taobh thiar dá chluasa' ('Snow is on the way when the cat washes behind his ears').

In general, it is important to distinguish between proverbial wisdom ('A sunny Christmas makes a fat graveyard' – 'Deineann

Nollaig ghrianmhar reilig bhiamhar'; meaning that unseasonally mild weather can hasten illnesses that can kill vulnerable people) and superstitious sayings ('A sunshiny shower never lasts half an hour' or 'If you leave your umbrella at home, it is sure to rain') which may include rhyming weather signs ('Níl Satharn sa bhliain ná go spalpann an ghrian' – 'There is no Saturday in the year that the sun doesn't shine': a common superstition is that the sun has to be seen at least once every Saturday; also 'A misty winter, a freezing spring, a sunny summer and a bountiful autumn' – 'Geimhreadh ceoch, Earrach reoch, Samhradh grianmhar is Fómhar breá biamhar'). Similarly, another widespread superstition in Ireland was the belief that weather conditions often changed on a Wednesday. Thus an old saying held that 'A storm does not last longer than Sunday, nor a swell longer than Wednesday' – 'Ní théann stoirm thar Dhomhnach ná rabharta thar Chéadaoin' (Ó hÓgáin, 2002).

Other weather signs that feature in Irish folk sayings emanate from the wind, mist and sea. To illustrate, consider the distinctions between various types of wind that are captured by the following triadic saying (see also chapter 8 on triadic proverbs). 'Trí bríos gála, trí gála feothan, trí feothan stoirm, trí stoirm airic' ('Three breezes make a gale, three gales make a winnowing wind, three winnowing winds make a storm, three storms make a hurricane'). These winds were often described in graphic terms. For example, a harsh wind was regarded as one that would 'skin a dog-fish' – 'Gaoth bhainfeadh an craiceann d'fhíoghach'. Ways of assessing the strength of a wind were also referred to in popular phrases. The saying that 'Dhádtrian gaoithe i gcrannaibh' ('two-thirds of wind is in the trees') indicates that the one can judge the power of a wind by examining its impact on the leaves of trees. The causes of winds were also considered. Strong winds were often attributed to the movement of the 'sí' or fairies – hence the name 'sítheadh gaoithe' (or thrust of wind) for whirlwinds (which were also known as 'deamhain aeir' or 'demons of the air'). Another cause of the wind was a mythical creature called 'Beartla na gaoithe' who had supernatural powers. In view of the possible malevolence of this creature, one should never look in the direction of a strong wind – but instead, pray that one will be unharmed by it (Ó hÓgáin, 2002).

Mist was also explored as a weather sign in ancient Ireland. Of particular concern was the 'ceo sí' or 'ceo draíochta' (the 'fairy mist') which could descend without warning, disorientating the person and perhaps signalling his or her impending death. Like the wind, the pattern of mist was held to foretell the weather. Thus 'Ceo soininne ar abhainn, ceo doininne ar chnoc' ('Mist of good weather on a river, mist of bad weather on the hill'). But this prediction is contradicted by another weather saying whereby 'Brothall – fionncheo ar thaobh an chnoic' ('A white mist half way up a hill is a sign of sultry weather to come'). In Scotland, an old expression suggests that 'A northern haar brings fine weather from afar'. The term 'haar' refers to a sea-mist which is associated with the North Sea coast of Sotland and England. It is usually associated with anticyclonic conditions and tends to herald the arrival of fine weather. In a related vein, a number of weather signs concerning the sea exist in Irish folklore. For example, bad weather is thought to be due when 'white roads' are visible in the ocean ('Doineann má bhíonn cúr na bhóithríní bána tríd an bhfarraige') or when the sea is very foamy at high tide ('Garbhadas amárach má bhíonn go leor cúir in aice an chósta, lán mára').

How accurate are traditional weather predictions? Although some of them have a solid basis in fact (as we have seen in the cases of a red sky at night and haloes around the moon), others are accurate for complex – and sometime wrong – reasons. This is especially true of weather signs detected from bird or animal behaviour. Consider the old rhyme 'Seagull, seagull, sit on the sand: It's never good weather when you're on the land' or its Irish equivalent 'Nuair a thiocfaidh na faoileáin faoin sliabh, tiocfaidh an stoirm ina ndiaidh' ('When sea-gulls fly inland, a storm will follow them'). Of course, the fact that seagulls huddle on the ground or fly inland may indeed presage bad weather because it may simply indicate that wind conditions at sea are *already* too strong or turbulent for the birds' comfort. Therefore, this behaviour may not be a sign of imminent bad weather but instead a reaction to it at that moment. Similarly, there is a weather saying that 'A cow with its tail to the west makes the weather best; a cow with its tail to the east makes the weather least'. Apparently, cows do not like the wind blowing directly into their faces and hence stand with their backs to the prevailing breeze. And since westerly winds typically bring mild weather whereas easterly winds bring cold or unsettled conditions, then a cow's stance may have some significance for weather prediction after all. Another example of a complex connection between weather and a natural sign occurs in the case of bird behaviour. Thus it has been said 'Nuair a sheinneas an chuach ar chrann gan duilleóg, díol do bhó is cheannaigh arán' – 'When the cuckoo sings on a tree without a leaf, sell your cow and buy bread'. The rationale for this saying is that if trees have not grown leaves before the cuckoo comes, then one will not have sufficient grass to feed one's cows so that one should stock up with other types of food (such as bread) instead (McWilliams, 1999).

Other Irish weather signs have a solid foundation. Consider the phrase 'Garraí na gealaí – báisteach' ('A garden around the moon means rain soon'). Usually, a ring or halo around the moon indicates the presence of cirrus clouds which precede low pressure weather systems containing moisture. Therefore, this rule of thumb is usually quite accurate. Also, the observation that low flying swallows herald the arrival of bad weather ('Fógraíonn áinlí ísle doineann' – a refinement of the proverb 'Is tuar fearthana alt áilleog' : 'A flock of swallows is a sign of rain') makes sense because before the arrival of rain, the air thins, causing birds to fly closer to the ground. Can good weather be predicted on the basis of perceived atmospheric conditions? According to some Irish phrases, it can – as is evident from 'Glór an easa i bhfad uait – dea-aimsir; drochaimisr más gár duit' ('Good weather is due when the sound of the waterfall is far away; a bad spell is due when the waterfall is audible') or 'Droch-chomhartha ar muir an léargas a bheidh go maith' ('If there is good visibility at sea, bad weather is coming'). Meteorologically, this latter insight seems plausible because it is known that as wet weather approaches, air pressure drops and dust particles in the air tend to settle on the ground – thereby facilitating enhanced visibility of distant objects. Similar sentiments are expressed in the old English saying 'A good hearing day is a sign of wet' (Giles, 1990).

An interesting type of weather lore is that which postulates an association between a particular day (usually a saint's feast-day) and a specific weather prediction. For example, in England, the feast of St Simon and St Jude (on 28 October) is associated with rainy weather. Thus 'On St Jude's Day, the oxen may play' indicates a prediction which seems to be well founded because the last week in October is statistically one of the wettest weeks of the year in the southeast region of England (Simons, 2005b, p. 28). Irish expressions of a similar kind are also evident. To illustrate, consider 'Every second day fine from my day on, said St Brigid; every day fine from my day on, said St Patrick' ('Gach re lá go maith ó mo la-sa, arsa Bríd; Gach lá go maith ó mo lá-sa, arsa Pádraig') (Partridge, 1978). The suggestion here is that from the first day of spring (1 February), which is St Brigid's Day, the weather should begin to improve. By St Patrick's Day (17 March), the improvement should be more noticeable. Likewise, in Britain, the legend of St Swithin's Day (15 July) suggests that on this day 'If it should rain, for forty days it will remain' but that 'If it be fair, for forty days 'twill rain no more' (O'Farrell, 2004). Of course, there is a grain of truth to this proverb because if a weather pattern has settled by mid-July, it is plausible that it will persist for some time. In passing, it is interesting to note that St Swithin (who died in 862) was a theologian who became Bishop of Winchester in 852 and died a decade later. Over a century later, in the wake of many miracles attributed to him, St Swithin's remains were scheduled to be moved to a new cathedral on 15 July 971.

Ní hé lá na báistí lá na bpáistí (The day of rain is not the day of children). St Patrick's Pilgrimage.

However, legend suggests that a storm raged on that day and rain fell
for forty days and forty nights afterwards – so the monks left him
buried in his original resting place. This torrential rain was
interpreted as a sign of the sadness of Swithin at the prospect of being
buried elsewhere. Similar weather superstitions associated with
saints' feast days are evident in other countries. For example, in
Scotland, St Martin Bullion is alleged to control the weather on
4 July (McWilliams, 1994). Another link between a specific date
and weather predictions occurs in the case of 'groundhog day'
(2 February) in the USA. On this day, it is believed that if the
groundhog sees its shadow, thirty days of winter remain. If not, then
spring should follow immediately. Unfortunately, this theory lacks
empirical support.

Having examined some weather lore that has a basis in fact,
let us now turn to those weather sayings that seem to make little
meteorological sense. For example, the old saying 'Rain before
seven, fine before eleven' is not accurate because research suggests
that precipitation in the morning is not a reliable predictor of a dry or
sunny afternoon. Likewise, the adage 'a mackerel sky, not twenty-
four hours dry' is tenuous at best. In addition, as we have seen with
proverbs in general (see chapter 1), weather expressions are often
contradictory. For example, consider the diametrically opposite
predictions of the following proverbs: 'When the fog falls, fair
weather follows; when it rises, rain follows' and 'When the fog goes
up, the rain is o'er; when fog comes down, 'twill rain some more'.

Scepticism about the validity of weather lore is not a recent
phenomenon, however. Thus McWilliams (1999) cites a quatrain
which expresses some disdain for natural weather divination:

Ná creid sionnach agus ná creid fiach
Agus ná creid comráite mná;
Pé moch nó déanach a eiríonn an ghrian
Is mar is toil le Dia a bheidh an lá

70

Do not believe the fox or deer
Nor women talking together;
Be it early or late the sun may appear,
Only God can dictate the weather

A variation of this disdain of predictive weather lore is reported by
Ó Cinnéide (1984):

Ní chreidfinn-se feannóg nó fiadh,
Nó go h-áirid briathra mrá
Luath nó mall a éireóchas an ghrian
Is mar is toil le Dia a bhéas a' lá

I would not believe the hooded crow or deer,
Or especially the word of women (old wives' tales)
Sooner or later the sun will rise
And the day will be as good as God wills it

WEATHER PROVERBS

Many weather proverbs are thousands of years old. Indeed, Aristotle
recorded some of them in his treatise *Meteorologica* as did his student, Theophrastus, in *Inquiry into Plants and Minor Works in Odours
and Weather Signs* (Kingsbury et al., 1996). Typically, weather proverbs have a distinctive structure whereby the text consists of a
conditional statement followed by a consequent assertion: 'If X, then
Y'. For example, 'April showers bring May flowers' or 'A wet March
makes a sad harvest' displays this structural pattern (Kingsbury
et al., 1996).

Despite their antiquity, weather proverbs have a controversial
status because they tend to be literal rather than metaphorical. For
this reason, some scholars (e.g., Dundes, 1984) doubt whether

weather lore can even be truly proverbial. This is a minority opinion, however, and Kingsbury et al. (1996) have no doubts that weather lore can indeed be proverbial. However, although they often contain vivid images, weather proverbs tend to be less figurative than other kinds of proverbs. Thus 'Leasú seacht mbliain brúcht mhaith sneachta' ('A good fall of snow is fertiliser for seven years') merely suggests that a heavy fall of snow will produce rich soil at a later stage. Accordingly, such proverbs are closer to predictive sayings than to metaphorical expressions. Nevertheless, many of the best known weather proverbs in English *are* metaphorical in nature. 'Make hay while the sun shines' could be taken literally by farmers – or it could be used to encourage any form of entrepreneurial activity or initiative. Likewise, proverbs such as 'One swallow does not make a summer', 'Lightning never strikes twice in the same place' or 'Every cloud has a silver lining' have several different layers of meaning.

Figurative interpretation is possible for certain Irish weather proverbs such as 'Cha dual grian gan scáile' ('There is not usually sunshine without shadows') or 'Is annamh earrach gan fuacht' ('seldom is spring without cold'). These proverbs are reminiscent of the English expression that one must 'take the rough with the smooth'. Another interesting proverb is that which has an optimistic theme despite a rather forbidding appearance. For example, consider 'Is mairg a báitear le linn na hanaithe, mar tagann an ghrian i ndiaidh na fearthainne' ('Woe to the person who drowns during a storm because the sun comes out after the rain'). Figuratively, the message conveyed here is that people should not give up hope during hard times because adversity eventually passes and things get better. In a similar vein, 'Níl tuile ná tránn ach tuile na ngrást' – an expression which is used to console people in times of trouble – proposes that no matter how many misfortunes befall a person, they will be overcome by God's grace. Likewise, the expression 'Tiocfaidh lá fós go mbeidh gnó ag an mbó dá heireaball' or 'A day will come yet when the cow will have a need to use her tail' is worthy of comment. The reference to the cow's use of her tail comes from the fact that on a fine day, a cow will swat flies with her tail. So, this proverb is intended as a riposte to people who complain too much about bad weather as it suggests that good weather may be on the way. Similar sentiments are expressed by the proverb 'Níl aon gaoth ná go séideann cóir do dhuine éigin' – 'There's no wind that doesn't blow in the right direction for somebody' – which has its English equivalent in 'It's an ill wind that blows no good', indicating that circumstances that are unfortunate for one person may be of benefit to another.

An unusual proverb with an ironic twist is the Wellerism (a quotation proverb involving a familiar quotation and its facetious sequel, such as '"one look before is better than two behind", as the man said when he fell into the well'; Williams, 1992) which says: '"Aimsir bhreá againn, mar a dúirt an bhean nuair a fuair sí a fear báite' ('"We have beautiful weather", as the woman said when she found her husband drowned'). This proverb is used as an ironic comment to make light of bad weather.

An Irish proverb which raises the issue of timing is that which says 'Ní hé lá na gaoithe lá na scolb' – or 'The windy day is not the day for thatching'. Taken literally, this proverb dates back to the time in Ireland when 'scollops', or slender wooden hoops made of willow or hazel, were used to fasten the bundles of straw required in thatching a roof. Obviously, windy conditions made such work futile and hazardous. At a figurative level, however, this proverb reminds us that *proactive* behaviour is always preferable to reactive solutions in dealing with a problem. In this sense, its sentiments echo the familiar expression that there is no point in closing a barn door after the horse has escaped or, as a traditional expression suggests, 'fál fa'n ngort a n-déigh na fóghala' – 'putting a fence around the field after the robbery' . Of course, it is entirely possible that the 'windy day . . .' proverb merely reiterates the Biblical proposition that 'to every thing there is a season, and a time to every purpose under the heaven' (Ecclesiastes, 3: 1).

Birds and animals feature in a number of Irish weather signs (Ó Cinnéide, 1984) and sayings (Rosenstock, 2000). Some of these animals – such as frogs and herons – are credited with an uncanny ability to presage either good or bad weather, depending on their appearance or behaviour. For example, 'Déanfaidh sé báisteach throm má thagann leipreachán an chlaí isteach sa chistin' – 'It will rain heavily if the frog comes into the kitchen'. Clearly, the 'leprechaun of the ditch' was a portent of short-term changes in weather conditions. For a longer range prediction, however, the reproductive behaviour of this animal was regarded as important. McWilliams (2005a) outlines the folk belief that when frogs spawn in the middle of a pond, a drought may be imminent. Conversely, when frogs spawn at the edges of a pond, they appear to have no fear of a water shortage so wet weather may be expected. Folklore also attributes prognostic significance to the colour of the frog's coat as well as its behaviour. Thus 'Gealbhuía bhíonn leipreachán an chlaí agus an tsoineann an teacht ach comhartha doininne is ea cóta dorcha a bheith air' – 'the frog is yellow for good weather but if his coat is dark, bad weather will come'. A variation on this piece of wisdom is the old English rhyme 'The frog has changed his yellow vest, and in a russet coat is dressed' (McWilliams, 2005a, p. 20). However, this observation seems to be accurate only because frogs change the colour of their coats as a *result* of changes in weather. In other words, this weather saying is retrospective rather than predictive. Curiously, this association between frogs' behaviour and changes in weather conditions is also evident in other countries. For example, mountain frogs in Kenya tend to croak when the temperature remains above zero degrees but fall silent when the temperature drops below freezing point (McWilliams, 2005a, p. 20).

Another weather sign derived from animal behaviour is 'Aimisr chrua thirim nuair a bhíonn an chorr éisc suas in aghaidh srutha chun na sléibhte: fearthainne nuair a ghabhann sí an abhainn anuas' ('When the heron swims upstream by the mountains, the weather

will be dry but rough: when she goes downstream, it will rain'). Wet
and windy days are also regarded as imminent when oyster-catchers
call ('Fliuch gaofar is na roilligh ag éagaoin'). Other birds to feature
in weather proverbs are swallows and robins (McWilliams, 1999).
Thus a flight of swallows may precede rain: 'Is tuar fearthainne ealt
ainleog'. In the case of robins, however, location was important in
signalling weather changes. For example, 'Má bhíonn an spideog
faoi thor ar maidin beidh sé ina lá fhliuch' ('if a robin hides beneath a
bush in the morning, rain is on the way'). On the other hand, 'Má
bhíonn sí ar an ghéag is airde, is í ag gabháil cheoil, beidh sé ina lá
maith' ('If she sings from the highest branch, it will be a good day').
The significance of a robin sitting high up on a tree is also conveyed
by the expression: 'Dea-shíon – an spideog ar bharr na gcraobh'.
Likewise, when a fox barks at night, it will be dry the following day
('Triomach chugainn nuair a dhéanann an sionnach tafann oíche'). A
change in weather can also be expected if bees are busy after sunset
('Beach ar saothar agus an ghrian faoi – athrú aimsire'). However, a
harbinger of bad weather is the sign of a seal travelling up the strand
away from the water: 'Drochaimsir má thagann an rón isteach i
mbéal na trá' or when a herd of cows lies down together in the middle
of a field ('Báisteach chugainn: tréad buaibh sínte in aice lena chéile i
lár páirce nach mbeadh fonn orthu éirí').

In this chapter, we showed that weather conditions provide a
familiar if somewhat neglected background to our everyday lives.
Indeed, the inherent unpredictability of our climate may explain the
enduring appeal of weather as a conversation piece among people in
Ireland. At a deeper level, we argued that a useful way of probing the
climatic tapestry of our lives is through the analysis of Irish weather
wisdom derived from various prognostic signs and proverbs. Having
described the factors which shape Ireland's temperate climate, we
mentioned two natural catastrophes of the nineteenth century – the
'night of the big wind' and the Great Famine – which entered folk
memory for future generations. After that, we explored various

weather observations, signs and superstitions. Finally, we examined the nature and significance of selected weather proverbs. Overall, we concluded that although many of our weather expressions are unreliable and contradictory, they are rich in allusion and provide some intriguing insights into Irish folk beliefs and practices.

5

Money, Markets and Land

'Nothing for nothing in Ballysadare'

INTRODUCTION

Proverbs are echoes of the past, drawn into usage in contemporary discourse. The strong echo of the past is worth reiterating, particularly in the domain of work, production and the role of the economy in people's everyday lives. At the time of writing, a leading and internationally respected magazine, *The Economist*, has published a lengthy article detailing the success story that is the recent Irish economy. Specifically, it asks how a country that 'was suffering from an awful cocktail of high unemployment, slow growth, high inflation, heavy taxation and towering public debts' in the 1980s, reinvented itself to create the level of growth previously known only in some East Asian economies, along with 'enviably low unemployment and inflation, a low tax burden and a tiny public debt'. That economic success story need not detain us here. However, its impact on our collective memory must be recognised. Furthermore, the transformation wrought by such a change inevitably reveals a good deal of our previously accepted 'truths' as historically contingent folk wisdom. There was a time, and indeed it was a long time, when Irish society was far from being the darling of Western economies, or a role model for small European countries, and was instead regarded as a particularly stagnant backwater of Europe. It had a rural, agrarian and peasant character and it is this very character, not the brash, self-confident services-industry economy, which Irish proverbs reflect.

77

What, then, are the chief social-psychological values of peasant societies? Joe Lee's (1989) socio-historical analysis of the Ireland of the past is widely respected. He notes the disastrous pattern of poor economic productivity of Irish society for most of the twentieth century, along with its low population growth. A society dominated by a powerful section of conservative 'strong farmers' and relying upon an astounding level of emigration as a necessary corrective to a stunted economy inevitably had some odd social values (at least seen from today's perspective). The perception, and indeed reality, that the size of the economic cake was fixed, meant that 'one man's gain did tend to be another man's loss' (Lee, 1989, p. 646). Thus, the stress on caution, and envious begrudging since 'keeping the other fellow down offered the surest defence of [one's] own position. It was difficult for an individual to rise rapidly in an agricultural society. . . except at his neighbour's expense' (p. 646). Holding on to land as a sure sign of status was also important. Thus, this chapter heading includes 'land' as a core issue at the root of Irish peasant concerns, and therefore Irish life. Battles for status often meant battles for land; and in a society of few opportunities, it also entailed relentless pessimism, bitterness, suspicion of others' wealth and envy, as well as thrift, born out of poverty and bordering on meanness.

Of course, Ireland was far from being alone in having a large poor peasantry or a more successful group of farmers sitting above them. For example, Italy, Poland, Russia, France and other European countries were also shaped ideologically to a great extent by their large rural populations as well as, in the case of three of them, large-scale migrations of peasants. Perhaps what made the Irish situation more intense was its political and geographical proximity to Britain, a powerhouse of European growth and technological change in the nineteenth century (see McNeill, 1982). British industry demanded the right to operate internationally, the end to tariffs beloved of weak domestic economies and ever greater freedom for employers and workers. Indeed its transformation from the world's greatest

78

slave-running and slave-selling nation in the eighteenth century to its role in the nineteenth century as a tireless opponent of slavery (even using the cannon of the Royal Navy to force the issue) reflects this restless, revolutionising energy. 'Where there's muck, there's brass' was the stereotypical proverb-slogan of the industrialists of Northern England: resources are appreciated for their potential. In Ireland, by contrast, where there was muck, there was status – resources were simply an end in themselves.

So what type of proverbs might one expect where the people are steeped in these begrudging peasant values? Sowell (1996) has highlighted the distrust of credit in such groups, as well as an ignorance of the power of loans to release value from assets. Furthermore, a deep antagonism towards historic middleman minorities such as the Overseas Chinese in Asia, Jews in Europe and Lebanese lenders in Northern Africa may also be present, along with a failure to understand their role in providing credit to peasant farmers. A 'scarcity value' instead will be applied to tangible and stable items such as land, immediate and liquid cash. The mercantilist pessimism around the nature of trade (seeing it as a fixed phenomenon rather than one with rich potential) should also be expected to feed through into common phrases and proverbs. A certain begrudgery, bitterness and envy might also be expected along with a caution about borrowing and a stress on saving.

In order to examine this idea, the chapter examines the content of Irish proverbs pertaining to issues like money, wealth (and poverty), land and investment. The hunch about their pessimistic nature will be assessed and an attempt made to provide a clear and overarching summary description of these proverbs as a whole. Following this, more subtle subsidiary analyses will be undertaken to examine whether alternative themes or discourses are at play. Recent social psychological research into a broad number of economic themes will be brought to the reader's attention in order to examine whether Irish proverbs also contained prescient insights about the human perspective on materialism. This will be in areas like equality, relative and absolute deprivation and the role of expectations. The similarity of Irish proverbs with proverbs drawn from other cultures, both agrarian and industrial, will be assessed. And finally, some light-hearted consideration will be given to what kinds of proverbs might arise from the new Ireland, with its economic success story and thereby altered social attitudes. A general conclusion will finally draw together the themes raised to offer the reader an understanding, in a nutshell, of money in Irish proverbs.

GENERAL THEMES SURROUNDING WEALTH IN IRISH PROVERBS

The *power of wealth and the persuasiveness of money* is a theme that emerges quite strongly and immediately from an analysis of Irish proverbs. From Williams (1992, p. 79), we find, 'money makes the horse gallop whether he has shoes or not'. That one can easily reach goals that are unobtainable without money is grittily apparent from, 'Sweet is the voice of the man who has wealth' (Gaffney and Cashman, 1974, p. 89). The general ease of life associated with wealth is frankly acknowledged: 'A heavy purse makes a light heart'. Not surprisingly, the motivational aspect of money is often translated into agricultural settings, although the brash materialism stills comes through: 'Money makes the mare go', 'money talks', or 'The man who pays the piper calls the tune' (all three from O'Farrell, 1980, pp. 66–7). Most unashamedly of all is, 'Cluinnidh an bodhar fuaim an airgead' ('The deaf will hear the clink of money', from MacDonald, 1926: p. 38, although it should be noted that MacDonald's collection reflects Scots Gaelic rather than the Irish tradition).

As noted above, despite the positive, if risky, role that money-lenders may have played in lending to farmers while they waited for harvest of market, *the fear of, and hostility to the money-lender* are palpable. 'The money-maker/lender is never tired' (from Gaffney and Cashman, 1974, p. 89) must have reflected the harried sense of peasants that they were being squeezed by rapacious middlemen. A proverb close in meaning is 'The hardest man to tire is the money-lender' (from O'Farrell, 1980, p. 66). There is interplay also between proverbs when it emerges that the unluckiest person to meet is not a 'red-haired woman' (as superstition would have said) but 'the man that lent you money' (from O'Farrell, 1980, p. 66). Again, the temporal rhythms of farmers' lives are reflected in many of the proverbs; for example, 'A month before harvest the merchant sells nothing but money' (O'Farrell, 1980, p. 67). The contradictory nature of proverbs is once again apparent though with the scorn of people towards those who refused to lend money: 'Is duine cóir é, ach na iarr a chuid' (or 'He's a "fine man" but don't ask him to share'). Furthermore, we also find another proverb, 'Ná toir iasad air an iasad' (literally, 'do not lend a loan'). Presumably, if there is an underlying theme here, it is that one should be willing to help out others with temporary loans or credit but one should avoid the taint of usury, i.e. lending for a profit. The problem, or course, obvious to any economist, but no doubt to shrewd peasant folk also, is that money has a 'time value'; this is the basis for the existence of powerful banks and financial institutions. From the perspective of small landowners, struggling to survive perhaps a short amount of time until the money from the harvest came in, the request for credit must have appeared trivial and its refusal – or worse, its granting but at high interest rates – must have appeared cruel and vindictive.

Simple anti-materialism is a strong theme, not surprising in a society dominated by Catholicism, and in which many transactions would still have been of a non-financial nature. To people on the fringes of market dealings, proverbs damning the growing tentacle-hold of notes and coins must have held a strong, emotional appeal. (In passing, we should note that the rulers of many European countries were also frustrated by the ways in which the iron laws of economics circumscribed their freedom to act and their self-declared absolute power. They could, by *fiat*, dismiss their debts but their creditors were unlikely to forget this the next time they needed to borrow money quickly.) The potential of rural people to be suckered into squandering their cash in the towns was keenly expressed in, 'The town leaves an empty pocket with people' (Williams, 1992, p. 79). The ability of money (or lack of it) to destroy a person is analogised to alcohol and its power in the proverb, 'Thirst after the drink and sorrow after the money.' (O'Farrell, 1980, p. 66). The hard-hearted, unforgiving nature of the cash nexus is nicely portrayed in 'As the money bag swells, the heart contracts' (O'Farrell, 1980, p. 67). Even more graphic is the somewhat scatological proverb, 'Money is the root of all evil but avarice is the compost' (O'Farrell, 1980, p. 67). And the possibility of happiness outside of or independent from money or material wants and cares also makes up part of this anti-materialist theme: 'Is fhearr na'n t-ór sgeul air inns aír choir' ('Better than gold is a story well told'). This proverb nicely illustrates both the non-material pleasures available to those without wealth while also providing an example of a social-psychological principle: where people feel that their social comparison with other groups will not favour them (those without money who compare themselves to the rich along a materialist dimension are unlikely to feel a great deal of satisfaction), a common strategy is to change the dimension of comparison, for example, they have the money but we have the soul, or they have the power but we have the spirit. A version of this is found in 'There is misfortune only where there is wealth' (Gaffney and Cashman, 1974, p. 89). And in more positive vein, we find, 'Ní raibh a dhóthain riamh ag éinne. Ach an té a bhí sásta lena raibh aige' ('No one ever had enough. Except the one who was happy with what he had', Fios Feasa, 1998).

A complementary theme to the anti-materialism one is what might be described as the *lot-of-the-poor* – simple sighs of the general injustice of life, as will be seen. (Or we might think of this theme as one of fatalism – see chapter 6 for discussion of a more general fatalism concerning people's health and mortality and the wry humour some proverbs express in this regard.) 'It's many a crush the poor get' (Williams, 1992, p. 79). Or with a greater sweep, and reflecting the very little cash available to the poor, 'Éirinn ar phingin; má tá, cá bhfuil an phingin?' ('Ireland for a penny, but where is the penny?') The disparity of rich and poor is never absent from discourse – 'A poor tinker would like to have a rich man's problems' (O'Farrell, 1980, p. 66). Or more simply, 'money taken, freedom forsaken', a comment that might be a universal reflection of the poor the world over – how penury apparently robs them of their autonomy. (Or might it specifically refer to taking the Queen's shilling and joining up in order to survive?) Another grim example of the lot-of-the-poor is 'Is é an bia capall na hoibre' (from Hickey, 2005), 'Food is the workhorse': in other words, malnourishment, not laziness, was typically the problem for the Irish peasantry.

Related to this theme is one that tries to illustrate to the poor the difficulty of building much capital from small amounts. This was of course true, but it also seems likely that such phrases would have had a soothing effect. 'A man of one cow – a man of no cow' or similarly, 'There's little value in the single cow' (Gaffney and Cashman, 1974, p. 89) or 'There's no use in shouting in the fair when you have nothing to sell' (Williams, 1992, p. 81).

The societies in which proverbs played the most important role tended to be ones where formal education was in short supply. There was no easy access to libraries, primers or best-practice guides. Thus, it is not surprising that proverbs should have an *educative/informative role*. This is easily visible in the area of finance and commercial transactions where a large proportion, perhaps even a preponderance, of proverbs are simply solid pieces of advice as regards money. 'A wet day is a good one for changing a pound' (Williams, 1992, p. 79). Caution, above all, and keeping your eyes peeled, are drummed home. 'Your eye is your mark, your pocket is your friend, let the money be the last thing you'll part with' (Williams, 1992, p. 80). One can imagine the fretting parent advising thus to the excited offspring heading to a market day or the town. Similarly, 'Before you buy, consult your purse' or 'Don't buy through your ears but through your eyes' and the very direct, 'taste and try before you buy' (all from Williams, 1992, p. 80). Or from MacDonald (1926, p. 48), 'Is fhearr a bhí leisg gu ceannach ná ruinnigh gu páigheadh' ('Hesitation in buying is better than delay in paying').

But it is not all caution: there is some shrewd advice on marketing one's goods. 'Mura mbeadh agat ach pocán gabhair, bí í lár an aonaigh leis' ('If you have only a buck goat be in the middle of the fair with him', Williams, 1992, p. 81). That is: get seen, be visible, advertise your goods. Or beware of the ups and downs of market conditions: 'Ná cuir do chuid uibheacha uilig in aon bhosca amháin' (Don't put all your eggs in one box', Williams, 1992, p. 81).

A related pedagogical theme is one which tries to warn people of the hard knocks and *brutal reality of the market*. These would all have served as good wake-up calls to even the dreamiest market optimist. 'Ní fhéadfadh sé a bheith ina phic is ina mhála' ('You can't have the hen and the price of her', Williams, 1992, p. 81), a version of course of the English, 'you can't have your cake and eat it [too]'). Untroubled business is not the norm either since, 'Cha deanar buanachd gun chall' ('There is no profit without loss', MacDonald, 1926, p. 39). And if you really want to know someone . . . ? 'Cha'n aithnich thu duine, gus am bi do ghnothaich ris' ('You will never know a man, until you do business with him', MacDonald, 1926, p. 39).

Finally, we should note the presence of another, perhaps unexpected, theme to be found within Irish proverbs concerning money, markets and land. This theme, quite at variance with those discussed above, is a *pro-market message*. This may reflect a powerful belief that despite the structural problems facing the great number of poor, that hard work and positive thinking will lift them out of poverty; or it may be simply an ideological message absorbed from a

84

Ná cuir do chuid uibheacha uilig in aon bhosca amháin (Don't put all your eggs in one box). Bird market, Dublin.

conservative Church and other powerful institutions. For example, we find the message that 'Gheibh pingin pingin eile' ('One penny gets another'), with the suggestion that quiet industriousness can pay off. Or in a different expression of pro-business sentiment, 'Can'n eil úaill an aghaidh tairbh' ('Pride is not against profit', MacDonald, 1926, p. 37). And MacDonald also finds some simple proverbs warning against idleness and praising the value of industriousness: 'Am fear a ni obair na thráth, bídh é na leth-thámh' ('He who does his work in time, will always have leisure time', MacDonald, 1926, p. 37) and 'Am fear nach cuir ri lá fuar, cha bhuan e ri lá teth' (He who will not sow on a cold day, will not reap on a warm day', MacDonald, 1926, p. 37). The message is clear: work hard and you can enjoy the benefits.

So, can the essence of Irish proverbs be captured? Is there an in-a-nutshell version? As we have noted in other chapters, it is clear there is not. What characterises proverbs is, at least partly, their flexibility. Most are simple and direct (although as we shall see below, often retaining a good degree of sophisticated insight) but taken as a whole or multiplicity, they have the capacity to provide an analysis or preparation for every situation, albeit often by recommending entirely contradictory courses of action. Thus the initial hypothesis of this chapter, that one could expect to find a bitterness and begrudgery about wealth and a suspicion surrounding the use of credit as well as towards moneylenders was not refuted *per se*. Themes of the pervasive corruptive power of money were noted as were those bemoaning the lot of the poor, the difficulty of breaking out of the poverty trap, fear and hostility to money-lenders, and the brutal unforgiving nature of market reality were certainly easily found. But along with those negative themes were some rather positive and unexpected ones around the potential to enjoy success, as well as neutral but shrewd ones offering general advice for the punter on market day.

The even more unexpected element within Irish proverbs in this financial domain is the degree of psychological awareness apparent in some of them. Within modern social psychology, the attention of many researchers has turned to the topic of 'relative deprivation'. This situation or phenomenon arises when somebody feels they are lacking something simply because they can see that others have it (rather than they are desperate to have it for its own sake, as with 'absolute deprivation'). The process was first formally noted by social psychologists during the Second World War, who were studying morale and levels of dis/satisfaction among the US Armed Forces. They observed that men in certain sections of the military, such as the Air Corps, were less satisfied than other groups such as the Military Police, despite having better objective conditions (more reliable and frequent promotions for example) than the Military Police; the problem was that they were comparing themselves to others in the Air Corps force who appeared to have much more than they did and felt relatively deprived, or deprived by comparison. So expectations about, and perceptions of, reality, social psychologists suggested, can play as important a role as 'actual' reality itself. A good deal of this subtlety can be found in Irish proverbs where the subjective element, somebody's perspective, is favoured over an 'objective' reading of the situation. For example, 'A penny in a poor man's pocket is better than two pennies in a rich man's pocket' (Williams, 1992, p. 80) is a nice statement of reasonably sophisticated economic and psychological approaches to motivation. Another proverb, 'A hut is a palace to a poor man' (Gaffney and Cashman, 1974, p. 89) is remarkably similar to Karl Marx's observation in *Wage, Labour and Capital* that 'a house may be large or small; as long as the surrounding houses are equally small . . . But let a palace arise beside the little house and it shrinks from a little house into a hut' (Marx, 1976, p. 35). Another nice comment on the gap between reality and perception is found in O'Farrell's collection (1980, p. 66) : 'a wage is the amount of money a man lives on; a salary is the amount he spends'.

Of course, such observations about the relative and social nature were not exclusive to modern day social psychologists, as the Marx quote reveals. For example, George Orwell, in his classic social history, *The Road to Wigan Pier*, written during the 1930s, captured it well when he wrote: 'Talking once with a miner, I asked him when the housing shortage first became acute in his district; he answered, "when we were told about it"' (quoted in Hogg and Vaughan, 2002, p. 386). What is interesting is that the concept of relative deprivation has usually been employed by researchers in seeking to understand popular uprisings such as the American, French and Russian revolutions. Thus it has been a *post hoc* device enabling social scientists to infer a mediating variable between unjust economic conditions and mass protest (it is no surprise then, that relative deprivation enjoyed its greatest levels of interest among social scientists in the US when riots broke out in mainly black urban ghettoes in the late 1960s and early 1970s, see Berkowitz, 1972). But is it not strange that the Irish peasantry, relatively politically quiescent and with essentially conservative political demands, should show an awareness of the potentially explosive sense of relative deprivation and relative injustice? Even the Land League protests were essentially of a limited nature, seeking not an egalitarian society in Ireland but simply the conditions (the famous 'Three Fs') for a stable peasant life to be made possible.

Social scientists have made one other major contribution to understanding how people respond to money and this is the study of public happiness (see also chapter 6 – the role of concerns about death and health in people's happiness). A number of insightful observers have noted the apparent disconnection between wealth and satisfaction. That is, despite increasing material prosperity and availability of goods among the populations of the west, there appears to be no commensurate increase in the level of happiness around. The failure of material well-being to translate into psychological well-being (or perhaps we should say the indifference of human restlessness to luxury) is a paradox requiring a clear explanation. For example, it flies in the face of the everyday experience whereby most people feel if they earned just a little more, they would be happy. Surveys show that rich individuals and rich societies are only slightly happier than poor individuals or societies. Similarly, when people are asked to recall the high points of the previous month or year of their lives, money usually struggles to make the top ten in importance while connection to others, autonomy and self-esteem tend to be at the top (as noted by Kenneth Sheldon and his co-workers, 2001). One explanation for the strange position of wealth in our psyches (seemingly all-important, yet on personal reflection and analysis, far less so) is the relativity argument touched on above. That is, increases in wealth only count in so far as, or relative to how others are getting on – and ideally, any increases we experience should tower above those of others. So while we noted above that the relative dimension is a feature of some proverbs, it appears that begrudgery is not an exclusively Irish phenomenon. The other explanation for the failure of money to satisfy, at least for very long, is the 'adaptation-level phenomenon' as framed by Philip Brickman and Donald Campbell in 1971. They argued that people adapt relatively quickly to their current level of achievements and failures. We try to succeed by aiming for some goal. If we fail, we feel unhappy. If we succeed we feel happy but only for a short while and then the satisfaction fades as we set our standards higher. Interestingly, this phenomenon is only weakly represented in Irish proverbs, if at all. It is not that the insight is especially modern. For example, Plato articulated a version of it when he wrote that poverty 'consists not in the decrease of one's possessions, but in the increase of one's greed' (quoted in Myers, 2002, p. 645). Rather, it requires a certain mobility and ladder of success for the adaptation-level phenomenon to occur: to be able to take things for granted is in fact a luxury and it was a luxury that the Irish peasantry, stuck in a poor and socially immobile stratum, never got to experience. Thus their language and their proverbs tended not to reflect this situation. And as noted earlier in the chapter, it increased the bitterness felt when those around them made even small improvements in their lives.

A COMPARATIVE ANALYSIS

How do Irish proverbs about wealth compare with ones from other countries? The collection edited by Jerzy Gluski (1971) is instructive here since it allows comparison of proverbs common in English, French, German, Italian, Spanish and Russian proverbs. Two sections focus on material-related issues: one is called wealth–poverty and the other is lending–borrowing. Examining first the wealth–poverty dimension, we find there are 33 proverbs considered to be in common usage among these European societies. The themes that emerge are actually quite similar to the Irish ones. There is the irresistible power of money to shape (and break) people's wills: for example, 'where gold speaks, every tongue is silent' (Gluski, 1971, p. 136), 'money will do anything' (p. 137), 'a golden key opens every door'. In a similar vein, the willingness of people to forgive the rich, or money anything, is also expressed in proverbs such as 'the rich hath many friends' (p. 139) or 'money has no smell' (p. 138; the German translation here is even more direct – 'Geld stinkt nicht').

There is also, though, the recognition that the absence of money is not necessarily a pleasant state: 'poverty parteth fellowship (friends)' or 'Poverty is a hateful good' translated into French as 'La pauvreté humilie les hommes'. The hard lot or life of the poor is further elaborated in proverbs like 'a poor man's tale cannot be heard'. The recognition of more subtle psychological themes like the gap between expectation and reality (highlighted in discussions around relative deprivation) is driven home by proverbs such as, 'nothing agreeth worse than a lord's heart and a beggar's purse' (Gluski, 1971, p. 141). There are also occasional anti-materialist messages such as 'content is more than a kingdom' (or 'contentment is the greatest of riches': p. 142). And there is a sober reminder to people to live within their means, 'cut your coat according to your cloth' (p. 143).

The theme of borrowing and lending is slightly different in tone from that found in Irish proverbs. There is no hostility to the lender himself, rather the proverbs tend to stress the weaknesses of those who seek out loans. 'He that goes a borrowing, goes a-sorrowing', 'the borrower is servant to the lender' (both from p. 148) and 'better to go to bed supperless than to rise in debt' (p. 149). If anything, the moral high ground slightly favours the lender – 'a good borrower is a lazy payer', 'creditors have better memories than debitors' (p. 148) and the slightly cavalier attitude of those not in ownership of a good is highlighted: 'a hired horse tired never'. There is a consistent warning that one is better off not getting involved with either borrowing or lending – 'lend your money and lose your friend' and 'better to go to bed supperless than to rise in debt'.

Overall, in contrast with these common European proverbs, it appears that the anti-materialist message is more commonly represented among Irish proverbs and there is more frequent hostility to moneylenders (whereas the European ones tend to warn against the loss of autonomy in owing to another). But both in common stress the difficulty of the lives of the poor while also containing the contradictory position that money cannot purchase happiness. The Irish ones tend also to include more subtle themes of modern social psychology than do the European.

PROVERBS – OF THE PAST?

It is clear that proverbs played a role in helping shape and maintain attitudes towards specific elements of wealth creation and financial transactions. In contemporary Ireland, it is irrefutable that society is ever more 'nakedly' dependent on cash relationships and that outside the family, most relationships already have been, or are tending towards, commercialisation. Irish success in the field of economics has meant lifestyles and financial habits once unimaginable are now merely considered a touch extravagant. For example, the average indebtedness of each household was recently reported to be at a record €134,615, or €44,000 per individual (*Irish Independent*, 13 July 2004 – 'Debt spiral warning as we borrow €120m a day', article by Pat Boyle. Collective Irish debt was reported at €247 billion in late 2005 – *Irish Times*, 1 December 2005). In the light of our new, possibly dangerously relaxed view of borrowing, one might expect that proverbs should be revolutionised in their role. If they are to act as the responsible watchdogs of the public psyche, a verbalised mass superego of sorts, ought not one now to see either the resuscitation of older proverbs or, even more interestingly, the emergence of new sources of advice for the Irish people? The imagination runs wild at the possibilities: 'a mobile phone battery in time saves nine [missed calls]', 'you can't have your cigarette and smoke it [indoors] too' or 'Taste and try before you buy. Or not. Whatever.'

And yet this does not appear to be occurring. The social, technological and economic changes appear, from anecdotal evidence, to be innovating slang and rejuvenating neologisms. But the proverb, with its gentle lesson, admonition or warning, quite simply does not seem to be cutting it any more. This is a large claim and should be accompanied by reliable evidence. Although such evidence is hard to come by the claim, though large, is probably uncontroversial. It is difficult to know why – perhaps the rate of change is simply too great and that a phrase which takes any time to spread among the public is doomed to be left at the starting blocks. Or that just as relationships between people have become increasingly commercialised, perhaps language, including proverbs, have also done so. It may be that the slogans and jingles of advertisements have replaced the use of phrases. Even if many of the proverbs in common usage were too fatalistic and saturated with resignation for our age, why was a process of evolution not observed whereby the more modern or flexible ones became favoured, while the rest were abandoned? But no: proverbs have declined *en masse*. And if one is to claim that in the proverbs of the past can be detected something of the Irish character and attitude towards money, what then can be said of the situation whereby proverbs are no longer used? That we have no especially distinctive attitudes towards money as a nation? This is quite possibly true. Indeed it would be unlikely, given the cultural penetration of Ireland by the US, UK and European societies, and the economic penetration of international capital, for the society to be any different from those countries. As an illustration, in the film, *Jerry Maguire*, one character's catchphrase is 'Show me the Money [Jerry]'. (The intended meaning incidentally, is, loosely, that you should put your money where your mouth is; and ideally, it should be a lot of money if you are really serious, since talk without financial backing is simply so much froth. Actions speak louder than words, especially where the action involves handing someone a large wad of cash). A number of years ago, I (M. O'C.) included this phrase in a book, as a section heading, in a chapter I was writing. It was immediately recognisable, certainly to younger readers of the text, and undoubtedly more so than a traditional proverb would have been at illustrating the same point. For example, 'obair duine gun chéill, Dol gun airgead do'n fhéill.' (A senseless man's procedure, Going to market without cash) (MacDonald, 1926, p. 128).

This is the issue alluded to in the introductory chapters – distinctive proverbs require a distinctive culture, economy and spiritual framework for understanding one's world. For example, in an interesting article, Barnes-Holmes, Cochrane, Barnes-Holmes and Stewart (2004) discussed that the idea of 'offering it up' (that is, of coping with life's disappointments and aches by simply enduring it and offering one's stoicism in the face of the pain as a tribute to God). Accepting that what happens is God's will ('do thoil a chur le toil Dé'), they suggest, is characteristic of a powerful form of Irish Catholicism. But it is informative that the authors add that this advice is reminiscent of what one's grandmother would suggest. (They go on to propose that such an approach to pain is actually helpful, and similar to the modern psychological technique of 'experiential avoidance'.) One would almost certainly not hear 'offer it up' as a solution to problems and discomfort in a modern setting. Instead newspapers have copious supplements outlining ways of combating, curing, avoiding, remedying and overcoming the thousand little knocks life gives us. And this is our modern Irish culture; it is one in which older proverbs, despite their wisdom, can no longer survive because they jar with the new international prevailing ideologies. Because in a society that has lost touch with its agrarian roots, and where so few live through the land, proverbs that rely on the patterns and rhythms of nature, and making one's living from appreciating those rhythms, simply lose connection to new speakers of Hiberno-English ('Earrach fad an deigh Cháisg, Fágaidh e na siabhlean fás', 'A long Spring after Easter will leave empty barns'). Empty barns? A long spring? And for that matter, Easter? Not a chance – supermarkets are all year round and all week open. Just show them the money!

6

Between Two Worlds: Irish Proverbs about Health, Happiness and Death

INTRODUCTION

At the end of the nineteenth century, people's reluctance to discuss the prospect of their demise led Jacobs (1899) to conclude that death was going out of fashion. Fortunately, Irish folklore and literature appear to have escaped this apparent taboo on the contemplation of one's own mortality. To illustrate, many Irish folk practices (such as 'sitting up' with or keeping watch over the dying person) suggest that death was an integral part of life and should be acknowledged publicly as a transitional experience to be shared with family and friends (Lysaght, 1995). Similarly, references to death are ubiquitous in Irish literature. Thus Leopold Bloom in *Ulysses* (Joyce, 1960, p. 139) proclaimed that 'The Irishman's house is his coffin' (p. 60). More significantly, many Irish autobiographies begin with accounts of death or dying. For example, the first words of Peig Sayers's life story (entitled *Peig*; Sayers and Ní Chinnéide, 1936) reveal that she is poised between two worlds: 'Seanbhean is ea mise anois, a bhfuil cos léi san uaigh is an chos eile ar a bruach' ('I am an old woman now, with one foot in the grave, and the other foot on its edge'). It is precisely this territory that lies between life and death that occupies us in the present chapter. Of course, such terrain has been explored previously by other writers. When Hugh Leonard revealed amusingly in *Home Before Night* (Leonard, 1979) that his grandmother had 'made dying her life's work', he highlighted the fact that many Irish households have grown up with a curious, tragic-comic perspective on life. Not surprisingly, popular expressions of this perspective in everyday language have attracted interest from anthropologists, folklorists, psychologists and psychiatrists who seek to understand the elusive 'Irish psyche'. Consider Warnes's (1979) analysis of the popular English phrase 'it could be worse', which is commonly used in Ireland. Briefly, he concluded that 'what happens is never the worst: on the contrary, what's worst never happens. Fate has unlimited credit and the interest is paid willingly and submissively' (Warnes, 1979, p. 331). We shall return to this idea of fatalistic beliefs later in the chapter when we explore some Irish proverbs about death. In the meantime, let us return to Hugh Leonard's account of his grandmother's titanic struggle to cross the boundary between life and death. Apparently, she used to stumble around the room 'clutching at the furniture for support and emitting heart-scalding gasps, as if death was no further off than the dresser or the settle-bed in which my uncle Sonny slept himself sober' (Leonard, 1979, p. 7). Arising from this vivid description, at least two questions arise. First, how far away *is* death for Irish people? In addition, what do Irish proverbs reveals about people's attitudes to, and beliefs about, ill-health and death? Interestingly, a wry perspective on this latter question comes from the Irish observation that 'a dying rannie often lives longer than a sound man'. To explain, the word 'rannie' in this expression comes from the term *ránaí* which, in Hiberno-English, means 'a thin, lanky person' or 'a delicate child' (Dolan, 2004). Similarly, other sayings indicate that people who are pre-occupied by illness are, paradoxically, often quite healthy. Thus the proverb 'Is fad saolta iad lucht múchta' (or 'Those who complain of ill-health are often long-lived') suggests that hypochondria may be a life-long vocation.

In summary, the purpose of the present chapter is to explore the nature and significance of Irish proverbs about health, happiness and death. As we shall see, much of Irish wisdom and folklore emphasised the importance not only of interpreting death as a natural part of life but also of involving the family and community in the grieving process (Lysaght, 1995). Before we explore Irish proverbs about death, however, we need to consider some popular expressions concerning health and happiness.

HEALTH AND HAPPINESS: THE
IMPORTANCE OF OPTIMISM

If proverbs are anything to go by, Irish people have always cherished their health. Indeed, the use of a salutation such as 'sláinte' (or 'health') as a prayer-like toast to one's companion before taking a drink is so widespread that it is almost taken for granted. Less popular today, however, is the longer expression 'Sláinte na bhfear. Is go maire na mná go deo' ('Health to the men. And may the women live forever'). Interestingly, the perceived value of health is highlighted by the fact that it was deemed to be preferable to riches. Thus the saying 'Is fearr an tsláinte ná na táinte' means 'Health is better than herds of cattle' (which, in the past, were visible signs of prosperity in Irish society). But what advice was offered for healthy living? Also, what strategies were advocated to cope with life's misfortunes?

Among the most important natural remedies recommended for various difficulties were laughter and sleep. Thus one Irish proverb proposes that 'Gáire maith is codladh fada – an dá leighas is fearr i leabhar an dochtúra' ('A good laugh and a long sleep are the two best cures in the doctor's book'). Similarly, it was held that 'A good laugh is as good as a day at the seaside'. Complementing such advice, the importance of developing a humorous disposition and an optimistic outlook on life was also emphasised. For example, it was widely believed that 'Maireann croí éadrom i bhfad' (or 'A light heart lives a long time') and that 'Dóchas liaigh gach anró' ('Hope is the physi-

97

cian of all misery'). Significantly, a considerable amount of research in positive psychology (an emerging movement in the discipline which is concerned with the factors that promote and sustain human happiness, flourishing and peak performance) has been conducted on the nature and implications of optimism (i.e., the expectation that things will work out positively for the person in the long run – seeing the glass as half full) in everyday life (see Haidt, 2006; Seligman, 2002). For example, such research has examined the relationship between people's 'explanatory style' (i.e., the way in which they habitually make sense of the things that happen to them in various situations) and their health and happiness. In general, studies in this field show that optimism is associated with both physical and mental well-being (Seligman, 1998). Specifically, when compared with pessimists (people who tend to blame themselves for their misfortunes and who have a negative expectation about the future – seeing the glass as half empty), optimists tend to report better physical health, a better quality of life, and more effective mechanisms for coping with stress. One possible explanation for such differences comes from research evidence which shows that when faced with pressure situations optimists tend to use 'problem-focused' techniques (making a plan, seeking advice from others) whereas pessimists tend to disengage themselves from the troublesome task or even deny that they are experiencing difficulties with it. Of course, there are many situations in which unbridled or unrealistic optimism can be dangerous (in taking up a risky sport or in making a hasty business decision) – especially when it comes close to wishful thinking. And so, modern research in psychology urges people to adopt a cautious or attentive form of optimism whenever possible. But how can people *remain* optimistic when faced with the challenges and setbacks of everyday life?

In the past, a popular method of coping with adversity in Ireland was to use the strategy of acceptance – as epitomised by the injunction to 'offer up' one's suffering (see also chapter 5). How helpful is this approach? Interestingly, as we mentioned in the previous chapter, Barnes-Holmes et al. (2004) concluded that acceptance-based strategies can increase people's tolerance for events that are perceived as physically and/or emotionally challenging. Indeed, in some circumstances, they appear to be more effective than traditionally advocated techniques like suppression (trying deliberately to forget the source of the distress) or distraction (trying to minimise its effects by thinking of something else) in such situations. Overall, patient acceptance is recommended when confronted with chronic or incurable sources of stress. Here, the advice involves 'Galar gan leigheas, foighne is fearr air' ('For a disease without cure, patience is best') or 'An nídh nach féidir a leigheas is éigin a fhulaing' ('what cannot be cured must be endured'). Patience is also regarded as 'a plaster for every wound' ('Is ceirín do gach lot an fhoighde').

THE SIGNIFICANCE OF SLEEP AND WHISKEY

Sleep was regarded as a useful index of health in Irish wisdom. For example, consider the saying that 'Tosach sláinte codladh' ('The beginning of health is sleep') and 'Deireadh sláinte osna' ('The end of health is a sigh'). These expressions are derived from an early Irish poem as follows:

> Tosach loinge clár,
> Tosach átha clocha,
> Tosach flaithe fáilte,
> Tosach sláinte codladh.
> Deireadh loinge í a bhá,
> Deireadh átha loscadh,
> Deireadh flaithe cáineadh,
> Is deireadh sláinte osna

99

The beginning of a ship is a plank,
The beginning of a ford is a stone,
The beginning of hospitality is a welcome,
The beginning of health is sleep.
The end of a ship is sinking,
The end of a ford is burning,
The end of hospitality is disparagement,
And the end of health is a sigh (Fios Feasa, 1998)

Problems in falling asleep were also explored. For example, the lack of sleep that often accompanies an illness was highlighted as a special concern. Thus 'Dhá dtrian galair an oíche' ('Two thirds of a disease is at night'). This observation is insightful as there is evidence in the field of 'somatic attention' (or people's sensitivity to their bodily symptoms) in psychology that people's awareness of their symptoms tends to become more acute at night – presumably because of the lack of competing sensations at that time. More generally, psychologists have raised the question of why we tend to experience a sudden 'worsening' of an ache or pain at night as the house grows still. In general, they attribute this phenomenon to the fact that when the external environment provides relatively little new information (as happens at night), our focus shifts to our own thoughts and feelings, thereby exaggerating the prominence of bodily sensations in our consciousness. Some support for this theory was provided by Pennebaker and Lightner (1980) who found that jogging around a small track repeatedly made people feel more tired than did jogging the same distance on a cross-country route in one direction only. Presumably, in this case, the monotony of running around the same terrain on the track caused athletes to shift their focus away from the outside world and on to their own sensations.

Another theme in Irish proverbs about health concerns the value of whiskey. Clearly, the curative powers of this alcohol were highly valued. For example, it was held that 'An rud nach leigheasann im ná uisce beatha, níl leigheas air' ('What butter or whiskey will not cure is incurable'). Another proverb extolling the merits of whiskey claims paradoxically that 'Whiskey when you're sick makes you well, whiskey makes you sick when you're well'. In passing, it is notable that whiskey was also prescribed as a soporific by folk-healers to help people overcome insomnia (Logan, 1981). Moving on, since 'sleep is the brother to death' ('Dearbhráthair don bhás an codladh'), let us consider some Irish proverbs about Irish people's attitudes to death.

DEATH

A number of Irish sayings tackle the theme of death. Not all of them are proverbs, however. Consider the following selection of curses. First, the phrase 'Cloch ar do chairn' (or 'a stone on your burial mound') indicates that the speaker cannot wait until the listener is dead so that s/he can put a stone on that person's cairn or burial site. Similar hostility towards the deceased is evident in the expression 'There'll be many a dry eye at his death'. Perhaps the worst curse of all, though, is 'Bás gan sagart ort!' – or 'May you die without a priest'. This insult was considered to be especially severe because the prospect of dying without receiving the Last Sacraments could jeopardise the eternal salvation of the soul of the deceased (Lysaght, 1995). Fortunately, not all 'death' sayings are as venomous as that one. In fact, they convey a variety of themes, ranging from the dark to the comical. These themes may be organised as follows.

Firstly, several proverbs emphasise the inevitability of death. Among this category are such expressions as 'Galar fada, ní abraíonn go síoraí bréag' ('A long illness never tells a lie'); 'Níl luibh ná leigheas in aghaidh an bháis' ('There is neither herb nor cure against death'); 'Chan fhuil lia ná leigheas ar an bhás' ('There is no physician or cure for death'); or 'Níor thug an bás spás do dhuine ar bith a riamh' ('Death never granted anyone a respite'). Likewise, it has been said that 'Nuair a thiocfas an bás ní imeoidh sé folamh' ('When death comes, it will not go away empty-handed'). Despite its inevitability, death was perceived somewhat sardonically in certain Irish expressions. For example, consider 'Sé an bás leigheas an duine bhoicht' – 'Death is the poor person's cure' or its equivalent expression 'Lia gach boicht bás' ('The cure for all poverty is death'). Clearly, these proverbs reveal a combination of humour and fatalism in the face of one's mortality. But what exactly do we mean by 'fatalism', and what are its psychological implications?

For psychologists, the term 'fatalism' involves an expectation that one's life is determined largely by forces outside one's control such as luck, fate or the influence of powerful other people. Alternatively, it can be defined as the belief that the course of one's life is predestined and impervious to personal influence. Psychological research suggests that fatalistic beliefs are usually associated with a passive outlook in life and with poor coping strategies for dealing with stressful events. Interestingly, Irish folklore is replete with references to fatalism. For example, Ní Fhloinn (1980) investigated beliefs about the apparent reluctance of Irish fishermen to help people who were found drowning at sea. She interpreted this superstition as an expression of a fatalistic outlook on death. This attitude is epitomised by such maritime proverbs as 'Caithfidh an fharraige a cuid féin a fháil' (or 'The sea must have her own') or 'Bíonn a cuid féin ag an bhfarraige' ('The sea must have its due'). According to Ó hÓgáin (2002), fishermen believed that it was unlucky to save a drowning man at sea because, in time, the ocean might take the rescuer in compensation for its loss. Such a belief might explain why expressions such as 'do b'é toil na farraige é' ('it was the will of the sea') were often uttered by fishermen in the wake of drownings. Interestingly, such superstitions are still apparent today, as in the case of the *Rising Sun* fishing vessel which sank off the Saltee Islands in Wexford in November 2005, leading to the loss of three lives. When the boat sank, two men were drowned but only one body was recovered. Sadly, a few days later, a local diver who had volunteered to search for the body of the missing skipper of the vessel also drowned at the scene of the accident. Curiously, in a radio report on this tragedy, a member of the fishing community in Wexford remarked fatalistically that the boat 'was meant to take three' (Hickey, 2005). Other maritime expressions provide similar insights into Irish people's attitude to death. For example, consider the proverb 'Bíonn súil le muir ach ní bhíonn súil le cill' – 'There is hope from the sea but no hope from the cemetery'. This expression reflects the popular belief that if someone were lost at sea, there would always be a possibility that s/he would return home some days later because fishermen often took shelter in isolated places when they were caught in storms at sea. By contrast, there is total finality about the burial of a body in the graveyard. Loss of another kind affected Peig Sayers (see beginning of this chapter), when she lamented the emigration of her children to America. In an effort to console herself, she remarked that 'Is fearr súil le glas na súil le huaigh' ('It is better to expect a release from imprisonment than a release from the grave'). In passing, it is notable that the practice of lamenting the departure of emigrants to the United States was part of a custom known in some places as the 'American wake'. According to this tradition, the finality of the departure of the emigrant was emphasised by equating his or her journey to the New World with that to the next world (Fitzgerald, 2003). In other words, travelling to America was regarded psychologically by those left behind as analogous to death. And so, on the eve of the emigration, the family and friends of the person in question held a party in his or her honour. This occasion ritualised the community's mixed emotions surrounding the emigrant's departure – happiness that s/he was about to embark on a new life elsewhere yet sadness that the emigrant might be irrevocably 'dead' to the community in the future as a return from such a distance abroad was unlikely. Interestingly, people who emigrated to Britain did not usually receive such a 'wake' in their honour because it was assumed that they could return to Ireland more easily than those who had emigrated to America.

Another perspective on Irish people's beliefs about death comes from an analysis of 'banshee' folklore. According to Lysaght (1998), the term 'banshee' (from the Irish 'an bhean sí' or 'otherworld woman') refers to a female supernatural being who was believed to presage death in certain Irish families either by her cry (a piercing wail) or her appearance (usually in the guise of an old woman combing her hair). In order to understand the nature and significance of this death messenger, however, some background information is necessary. Briefly, a belief in an 'otherworld' community was common in ancient Ireland, as it was in many other countries. The members of this supernatural community were called the 'sídh' (or 'sí') (Ó hÓgáin, 2002). Out of fear or respect for these beings, however, they were referred to obliquely using circumlocutory terms such as 'na daoine maithe' ('the good people') or 'na daoine uaisle' ('the noble people'). Such respect for the 'otherworld' is still apparent among contemporary farmers in Ireland, many of whom are reluctant to knock down or plough under 'fairy forts' (circular mounds ringed with trees) on their land. Strictly speaking, however, the banshee was not a member of the 'sí' community (Lysaght, 1998). Instead, she was regarded as a solitary woman whose cry (described variously as a 'wail', 'keen' or 'lament' which was so loud that it could even be heard by deaf people) was a signal that death was about to strike in a community. Typically, this cry was heard near a person's house when s/he was fatally ill and close to death. It was rarely heard when death occurred unexpectedly, as in the case of accidents. Viewed from the perspective of modern psychology, perception of the banshee's cry could be explained by the tendency for people who are tired, anxious or emotionally upset (as a result of looking after a sick relative) to be especially susceptible to portents of the future. For example, the cry of a crow, an owl, a vixen or rutting deer at night could easily be mistaken for the wail of a supernatural being such as

Nuair a thiocfhas an bás ní imeoidh sé folamh (When death comes it will not go away empty-handed). Carndonagh Cross, County Donegal.

a banshee. This type of perception is even more likely when it occurs at night in poorly illuminated, remote rural areas.

A number of theories about the origin of the banshee have been proposed. One account suggests that she was a penitential being – perhaps a former keening woman who had been condemned to continue lamenting the dead eternally as a form of punishment for neglecting some aspects of her duties while she had been alive. Another theory speculated that she was an ancestral guardian spirit or the ghost of a woman who had occupied a kinship with the bereaved family in the past. Whatever her origin, the banshee played an important part in people's attitudes to death as she shared in the grief of the relatives and friends of the dead person through her wailing. It is important to point out, however, that she differed from a human keening woman in one significant respect – namely, that she was a foreteller of death rather than someone who lamented the passing of a person who had died. Thus as Lysaght (1998) observes, the banshee was rarely heard at wakes as these occasions were the places where human keening women performed their duties. In passing, it is also notable that the act of lamentation at wakes was usually performed by elderly women – apparently on the grounds that such people had generally experienced so many of the vicissitudes of life at that stage that they could readily empathise with the grief of the bereaved (Lysaght, 2001). One of the purposes of lamentation, therefore, was to provide a relatively brief yet ritualised opportunity to vent one's grief over the death of a loved one.

Psychologically, supernatural messengers like the banshee fulfilled at least two psychological functions for Irish people in the past (Lysaght, 1998). In order to understand these functions, it is necessary to examine the question of who received the death message – and who did not. To begin with, the appearance of the banshee heightened people's awareness of their own mortality. But there is an interesting twist to this idea. To explain, a key tenet of banshee beliefs is the idea that she will not appear to the person who is destined to die.

By implication, an encounter with a banshee was paradoxically comforting to people because it convinced them that they themselves were safe from imminent death. Of course, this relief was scant consolation for the worry about which of one's relatives was likely to die. But the illusory presence of the banshee may have helped the family of a dying person to prepare for and rationalise his or her departure. This possibility was especially likely if the dying person had experienced a long and painful illness from which death would be a merciful release. Therefore, as Lysaght (1998, p. 67) remarks, 'the death foreboding conveyed by the banshee could be of great psychological benefit to those attending the death-bed'. Specifically, when a death was imminent, there was 'a need for a messenger who could spread the news speedily, and folk imagination serviced the need by creating a being who could communicate the message even before the event had taken place' (Lysaght, 1998, p. 69). Thus as news circulated that a banshee had been heard close to the home of a gravely ill person, friends and neighbours would have been persuaded to visit him or her, offering moral support and practical help with domestic chores such as feeding the farm animals, looking after the land or taking milk to the creamery. Another psychological benefit of the appearance of the banshee was that it probably helped people (whether relatives or friends) to address any long-standing disputes or other unresolved issues that they might have had with the dying person. In other words, the banshee's cry may have prompted a death-bed reconciliation between the dying person and his or her erstwhile foes. This act of reconciliation was known as performing 'maith in aghaidh an oilc' (or 'returning good for evil') (Lysaght, 1998). In this regard, another proverb suggests that reconciliation is of paramount importance ('Ní rachaidh rogha ó réiteach' – 'there is a solution for everything'). Overall, Lysaght's analysis of banshee beliefs highlights the *communal* nature of the experience of death in traditional Irish society. This conclusion reminds us of the wisdom of the proverb 'Ar scáth a chéile a mhaireas na daoine' ('People live in one another's shadow').

A second theme among Irish proverbs is that death is largely even-handed, affecting people equally regardless of their age ('Níl fhios cé is luaithe, bás an tseanduine ná bás an duine óig' – 'There is no knowing which comes sooner, the old person's death or the young person's death') or material circumstances ('Ní bhíonn póca ar aibíd' – 'There is no pocket in a shroud/habit'). This latter proverb reminds us of the English phrase 'you can't take it with you' and conveys a certain disdain for the pursuit of wealth. A variation of the former saying is a proverb which suggests that one cannot always be sure that an older person will die before a younger one. Thus 'Ní túisce craiceann na seanchaorach ar an bhfraigh na craiceann na caorach óige' ('The skin of the old sheep is on the rafter no sooner than the skin of the young sheep').

A third theme of Irish death proverbs is a religious outlook on one's mortality. In these sayings, the emphasis is placed on the consolation to the bereaved that stems from the apparently inexhaustible supply of God's grace. To illustrate, 'Imeoir-se is imeod-sa as an áit seo, is beidh aiteann ag fás inár ndiaidh, Imeoidh a dtiocfaidh is a dtáinig riamh, Ach ní imeoidh na grástaí go brach ó Dhia' ('You and I will go away from this place, And furze will be growing after us, All who will come or who have ever come will pass, But the graces will never go from God').

Fourth, the insignificance and relative brevity of life are characterised by proverbs which contrast its transience with the more enduring aspects of natural phenomena. For example, 'Maireann an chraobh ar an bhfál, ach ní mhaireann an lámh do chuir' ('The branch lives on the hedge but the hand that planted it is dead'). Another example of this idea is the saying that 'Is beag an rud is buaine ná an duine' (or 'Few things are more permanent than the person').

Fifth, a number of proverbs address the theme of how people contemplate death. Included here are sayings which explore the way in which one's perspective on death may be influenced by one's age and one's emotions. For example, consider the observation that older people tend to think about their mortality more than do younger people: 'Bíonn an bás ar aghaidh an tseanduine agus ar chúl an duine óig' ('Death is in front of the old person and at the back of the young person'). Also, the possibility that the prospect of death can generate paradoxical emotions is captured by the proverb 'Síleann do chara agus do namhaid nach bhfaighidh tú bás choíche' ('Both your friend and your enemy think that you will never die').

Sixth, the fact that one never knows where or when one will die is expressed by the saying that 'Níl a fhios ag an duine cá bhfuil fód a bháis' ('Nobody knows where his or her sod of death is'). This idea of a belief in 'fód an bháis' (or 'the sod of death') is noteworthy. According to Ó hÓgain (2002), many people believed that a particular sod of earth was predestined for them. In other words, we shall all die on our own 'sods'. This fatalistic belief may have helped people in the past to rationalise and come to terms with a sudden or tragic death such as the loss of a child in an accident.

Seventh, some possible gender differences in the experience of death are hinted at by the proverb that 'Deireadh fir a shuan, is a bhean á faire féin suas' ('A man's end is his rest where his wife watches by herself'). Apparently, this saying captures an old Irish folk belief that whereas men allegedly drift off quietly on their deathbeds, women are supposed to resist death by staying awake for as long as possible. Figuratively, this proverb has also been interpreted as a comment on the tendency for men to fall asleep after sexual activity while their female partners remain awake (Fios Feasa, 1998). A harsher saying about death, tinged with misogynistic black humour, is evident in the quotation proverb which suggests that 'Sea, tá an méid sin de ghnó an earraigh déanta agam, mar a dúirt an fear taréis dó a bhean a chur' ('Well, I have that much of the spring work done, as the man said when he had planted his wife'). This saying was sometimes used after a man has finished a long job. It involves a play on words generated by the fact that the term 'cur' can mean either 'buried' or 'planted' in Irish. Emotional aspects of grief are explored as an eighth theme of Irish death proverbs. For example, could there be any emotion worse than that of losing a loved one? According to one proverb, such emotions exist, but often lead to favourable outcomes for the person afflicted by them. Thus 'An rud is measa leat ná bás, is leas dhuit go minic é' ('What seems worse than death to you is often for your good').

So far, we have examined Irish people's attitudes to, and beliefs about, death through their proverbs and folklore. But traditional behavioural customs surrounding death are also illuminating. In this regard, consider the tradition of the 'merry wake' in Ireland (Lysaght, 2001; O'Connor, 2003). This practice is believed to have been commonplace in Ireland at least as far back as the seventeenth century and seems to have continued until the early years of the twentieth century. During that era, when a person died, his or her body was laid out to be 'waked' at home until the remains were taken to the church on the evening before the day of the burial. At the wake, people lamented and prayed for the deceased and paid their respects to his or her family. Usually, the wake lasted for more than a night and, after the initial prayers were said, alcohol and tobacco were provided for the guests. In addition, a variety of 'wake amusements' were held (see Ó Súilleabháin, 1967). For this reason, most wakes were not solemn occasions but were regarded as social functions in which singing, dancing, storytelling and game-playing occurred. Given such festivities, is it any wonder that death was perceived somewhat ambivalently? For example, consider the proverb 'is minic a ligeas béal na huaighe rud chuig béal na truaighe' – 'the mouth of a grave often gave something to the mouth of the poor'. Of course, not all wakes were lively events. The death of a young parent was invariably regarded as a sombre occasion (Lysaght, 2005). Nevertheless, the majority of wakes were raucous occasions. It is hardly surprising, therefore, that the Christian Church authorities were moved to condemn boisterous wake activity on the grounds that it not only diminished the sanctity of death but was also a source of bad example for young men and women. In this regard, as late as 1903, the Bishop of Ardagh and Clonmacnoise apparently issued an order forbidding unmarried men and women to attend wakes between sunrise and sunset (Kiberd, 1993). Among laypeople, however, wakes were eagerly anticipated as they were often merrier occasions than weddings. This contrast is captured by a well-known joke: 'What is the difference between a wake and a wedding? One less drunk!' (Edwards, 2004). In general, young people tended to look forward to the wake of an elderly neighbour or relative as it afforded them a rare social outlet. Strange as it may seem, cards were some-times put into the hands of the corpse, a pipe stuck into his or her mouth – and, occasionally, the corpse was taken on to the floor to join the dancing! (Ó Súilleabhain, 1967). Among the reasons advanced for this curious custom were the theories that it placated the dead, was the last occasion on which the deceased and the living could share the same social occasion, and/or was an effort to ease the sorrow of the relatives. And so, this 'carnivalesque-type behaviour' highlights the paradox of the Irish wake – the fact that it was a solemn yet festive occasion which provided a psychological means of 'incor-porating the deceased into the ancestral otherworld' (Lysaght, 2001, p. 267). Intriguingly, another feature of the wake tradition is the belief that 'keening' (a term which is derived from the Irish word 'caoin', meaning 'to cry') should not take place immediately over the body of the deceased in case the Devil was roused by the sound and captured his or her soul. It is interesting to note this practice of keening features in another proverb which emphasises the impor-tance of acting in time: 'Ní haon mhaith a bheith ag caoineadh nuair a imíonn an tsochraid' ('There is no point in keening when the funeral has moved off' – indicating that there is no point in being sorry after the event). The point here is that in order to be effective, keening has to be performed in the *presence* of the body of the deceased (Lysaght, 2005). Although the practice of waking the dead in this fashion has virtually disappeared, some remnants of this tradition remain in contemporary Ireland in the custom of providing food and refreshments for mourners who visit the family home of the deceased person after his or her funeral – or who gather in a local bar/hotel after the event.

Overall, wakes fulfilled a variety of spiritual, psychological and social needs for Irish people in the past. Spiritually, they offered a ritualised way to negotiate the path between life and death. In this regard, festive waking was a ceremonial custom which combined elements of pagan beliefs and those of Christianity. An example of a pre-Christian superstition associated with waking was the belief that the doors and windows of the dead person's house should be opened in order to set his or her spirit free. It is possible that this attempt to liberate the soul of the deceased is connected with a custom that is still prevalent among members of the Travelling community today. Briefly, this custom stipulates that the caravan of the deceased should be burned in order to facilitate his or her journey to the afterlife. Next, at a psychological level, wakes provided a convenient temporary distraction for the family, thereby helping them with the bereavement process. The associated revelry also reminded people that life should be celebrated – even as one contemplates death. Finally, a family could enhance its prestige and reputation in the community by holding a large wake for a one of its deceased members. Thus the expression 'like snuff at a wake' epitomises the lavish generosity that was provided by the bereaved family for visiting sympathisers.

In summary, Irish literature and folklore contain extensive references to the mysterious terrain that separates living from dying. In this chapter, we explored some parts of this terrain not only through the prism of Irish proverbs (about health, happiness and death) but also through certain folk practices. In general, the proverbs that we analysed contain some surprisingly modern advice (for example, on the value of optimism) as well as interesting insights into people's beliefs about death. In particular, Irish wisdom and folklore emphasised the importance of interpreting death as a natural part of life and also of involving the family and community in grieving the loss of loved ones.

7

Interpersonal Relationships

'Níl aon leigheas ar an ngrá ach pósadh'
'The only cure for love is marriage'
(MacCon Iomaire, 1988, p. 108)

INTRODUCTION

While the chapter title is focused on interpersonal relationships and their treatment in Irish proverbs, the reader may (or may not) be surprised to find that it was really only in the context of marriage that interpersonal relationships were 'proverb-ed' in Ireland. This was of course because until relatively recently in Irish society, matters related to sexuality or indeed romance were only – and even then reluctantly – dealt with in common parlance within the institution of a church-approved marriage (although some historical analyses suggest that the variety of sexual contracts or lifestyles open to women was probably far wider in the early nineteenth century before religious and economic changes curtailed them enormously – see for example McLoughlin, 1994). Despite the Church's lauding of marriage, the cynicism of many Irish proverbs towards the institution [of marriage] and in particular towards the role of women within that institution has been noted and contrasted unfavourably with the idealised and hyper-romantic imagery of Irish love songs. A fairly typical example of the former is 'Bíonn a dteanga ina bpóca ag an mná go bpósann siad' ('Women keep their tongue in their pocket until they marry' – MacCon Iomaire, 1988, p. 100) – and of the latter, 'Is folamh, fuar teach gan bean' ('Empty and cold is a house without a woman' – 1988, p. 99).

THE HARSHNESS OF IRISH PROVERBS

Clearly, the passage of time plays an important role so that the power structure of domestic life in the past inevitably differs from the contemporary world (see below for a more detailed discussion of the Irish social structure of the past from which most proverbs arose). Even if political correctness were set to one side, the jarring negative proverb 'Trí ní gan riail, bean, muc agus múille' ('Three things without rule, a woman, a pig, and a mule' MacCon Iomaire, 1988, p. 99) – could not comfortably be used in any but the most ardent woman-hating setting today. (We note in chapter 8 how the specific triadic or tripartite structure was widely used in proverbs critical of women.) The autobiographical book, *Peig*, makes clear that the idea of romantic love, as opposed to, say, familial or religious devotion, was simply absent from nineteenth and early twentieth century peasant life – for example, as Peig recalls, 'bhí mo rogha de dhá chrann ar mo bhois agam, is é sin pósadh nó dul in aimsir arís' (Sayers and Ní Chinnéide, 1936, p. 124). Sociologists have suggested that the kinds of relationships, or more precisely the kind of marriages, typical of traditional societies tended to stress authority and hierarchy, with the men enjoying the overwhelming share of formal decision-making power. One can imagine that in an attempt to challenge this patriarchal status quo, women had to employ strategies of resistance carefully; inevitably this must have generated a counter-reaction, such as accusations of shrewishness, encapsulated in the proverb above. Given this context, it is not surprising to find that many of the more extreme anti-woman comments were related to the domain of spending and financial power. For example, 'Imíonn an spré is fanann an breall ar an mnaoi' ('The dowry disappears but the woman remains a fool') (Fios Feasa, 1998, section 34, no. 16).

Thus, it seems likely that proverbs, their popularity and usage were discursive or conversational weapons in a tough sex war in pre-modern Irish society. It was tough precisely because it was over life-and-death issues like money. Sugary confectionery would have been a tremendous luxury at the time; so too, conversation and idiom inevitably reflected the harshness of life – schmaltzy and sugary proverbs were a superfluity and an indulgence too far when fundamental struggles over power and resources between the sexes were under way. The themes of money and resources recur in 'Gach ní daor, mian gach mná' ('Every expensive thing, the wish of every woman' – MacCon Iomaire, 1988, p. 99). Given the simplicity, poverty and parsimony of Irish households and tastes in the late nineteenth and early twentieth century, this last proverb looks laughably wide of the mark. However, with the understanding that economic shortages made any resource or surplus relatively precious, the proverb becomes more meaningful. Yet another example of the materialist element underlying Irish proverbs is given in 'Ón lá a bpósfaidh tú, beidh do chroí I do bhéal agus do lámh I do phóca' ('From the day you marry, your heart will be in your mouth and your hand in your pocket' – MacCon Iomaire, 1988, p. 103). Of course, some of the antagonism towards marriage must have been based on the large families that usually followed, with all the corresponding pressures on hard-pressed parents.

Proverbs were at least partly a propaganda tool, presented as a truthful generalisation but favoured by men to keep women 'in their place', to hem in their power in a domestic context. It is interesting that analyses of propaganda have often found that at its most extreme, it tends to rely on animal imagery, in order to dehumanise its target (for example, American attempts to portray the Kaiser during the First World War as the 'Beast of Berlin' or Soviet poster portrayals of German soldiers in the Second World War as rabid wolves). The reader will have noted above the use of animal imagery (pig and mule) in a proverb related to the married woman; it is not an isolated case. Another example is 'Is dána muc ná gabhar ach sháraigh bean an diabhal' ('A pig is bolder than a goat but a woman surpasses the devil'), Mac Con Iomaire, 1988, p. 99. Again, and to the modern ear especially, the message is unnecessarily malevolent and ill tempered, its extremism undermining its supposed 'humorousness' and revealing the more likely intention to control. As is the nature of most propaganda, the aim of the user and creator was not a realistic portrayal of life; rather it was, where necessary, a vicious caricature. Thus 'Ní céasta go pósta agus ní féasta go róstadh' ('There is no feast till a roast and no torment till a marriage', Williams, 1992, p. 121) is notable more for its unnecessary fervour than its accuracy. Similarly, 'Díg gach dí an mheadg más sean, Díg gach crainn an cárthainn glas, Ach a ngíg go léir drochbean' ('The worst of drinks is whey when old, the worst of woods is green holly, but the worst of all is a bad woman') from Fios Feasa, 1998 – section 29, 1).

Ironically, for many of the young women matched into relationships with men thirty or forty years their senior, as was common when the 'strong' farmer dominated Irish society, the relentless anti-marital cynicism might actually have been an accurate reflection of the experience of married life. It is likely that many young women, again fairly powerless once their dowry had been paid over, felt only too keenly the truth of the proverb, 'Más maith leat tú a cháineadh, pós' ('If you want to be criticised, marry' – MacCon Iomaire, 1988, p. 112), given her institutional position of powerlessness as well as the defencelessness against husbands who may have been abusive in many ways. What is perhaps surprising is the one-sided degree to which relationships between the sexes are portrayed by proverbs. Gershaw (1998) has argued that proverbs, based as they are on common sense, tend not to be predictive but to explain behaviour *after-the-fact*. Thus, proverbs as a whole normally require a certain elasticity, as we have noted many times throughout this book, so that they can 'explain' both examples and counter-examples of particular kinds of behaviour – classic examples in English include 'Opposites attract' and 'Birds of a feather flock together'. Or indeed, as an Irish proverb puts it, 'Ní sáruighthear na seanfhocail' ('Proverbs cannot be contradicted', from Gaffney and Cashman, 1974, p. 77). So, it tells us a good deal about Irish society of the past that proverbs expressing the positive aspects of marriage are so rare.

PROVERB-COUNTING

What importance did interpersonal attraction hold for members of Irish society in the past? How much of their time was consumed with thoughts of love, lust, romance, partnership or companionship? Of course, it is impossible in a literal way to answer these kinds of questions. However, proverbs and analyses of their use allow a psycho-historian the possibility of a kind of time travel back into the past to assess the passions (or their absence) of previous generations. At the very least, simply grouping and counting the different kinds and categories of proverbs used should offer the investigator some sense of the people's priorities. This method is, of course, far from perfect as we have no way of knowing if the proverbs listed by collectors and archivists represent an exhaustive list of all those used. In fact, they almost certainly do not; regardless of the thoroughness of the researcher, inevitably those proverbs compiled in various indices that have survived are more likely to originate among more literate and probably more sociologically 'advanced' communities. And more worryingly, we have no way of knowing, with any degree of confidence, the varying levels of usage of any proverb (although there are now analyses ongoing of actual usage in vast corpora of written and written language); the assumption of even or uniform usage can hardly be tenable. Nevertheless, and with these caveats in mind, we can examine the numbers of proverbs devoted to issues of love and relationships and compare them to the space dedicated to other themes. Gaffney and Cashman's list contains 1,106 proverbs (excluding triads, see chapter 8 for a discussion of these specialised form of proverbs), drawn from various sources; they classified them into 188 categories, some of which were inevitably arbitrary (for example, 'equality' and 'inequality' as separate categories). What proportion of these might we expect to be taken up with the topic of love? What percentage might be reasonable, what might be indifferent or what would look obsessive about the topic (always assuming that people talk more about the things they care about)? In fact, we find that 18 proverbs are categorised as relating to the topic of love. This percentage appears to favour the indifference position – less than two per cent. However, this is a little unrepresentative – because there are so many classifications, the general issue of interpersonal relationships actually appears under a number of different guises aside from that specifically of 'love'– it also can be found under 'beauty', 'chastity', 'courtship', 'friendship', and of course, 'marriage'. If we use this broader definition of the topic, the number of proverbs now included totals 80 (with 'friendship' particularly important, having a tally of 31), which makes up a more impressive 7.2 per cent. If this still looks low (and it is also interesting that people found it easier to frame and presumably use proverbs around friendship than around 'courtship' which has only two entries – probably a sign of a sexually conservative society), then it should be noted that no other topic exceeds this in terms of frequency. In Table 7.1 below, the top ten topics, by number of proverbs, are listed. Looking at this table, it is certainly fair to say that interpersonal relationships are not noticeably neglected, particularly as some of the proverbs falling into the 'women' category are also related to love or sexuality, although normally from a male perspective, such as 'More hair than tit, like a mountain heifer' (Gaffney and Cashman, 1974, p. 92).

The smaller but more recent compilation by O'Farrell (1980) categorises proverbs into a set of 75 categories. Four of these categories overlap with those in the Gaffney and Cashman (1974) set – beauty, love, friendship and marriage – but there is no specific category for example for 'chastity'. There is, however, a category called 'company', not included in the earlier book. O'Farrell's book includes 1,083 proverbs in all. Of these, 29 (or less than three

Table 7.1 *Top ten topics, by number of entries, covered by Irish proverbs, as cited by Gaffney and Cashman (1974)*

Proverb classification	Number of entries
Friendship	31
Women	31
Marriage	22
Poverty	21
Alcohol	20
Experience	20
Caution	18
Health	18
Love	18
Nature	18

per cent) are directly related to the topic of 'love'. However, as before, if we include related or overlapping classifications such as beauty, friendship, marriage and, most loosely, company, then we find that the proportion of proverbs broadly dealing with interpersonal relationships totals 102 or almost 10 per cent of the total. O'Farrell's categorisations seem less unwieldy than the Gaffney and Cashman ones. The tabulation of the top ten issues, based on the number of proverb inclusions, is presented below (Table 7.2). The categorisations in Table 7.2 seem intuitively to capture more (than those of Table 7.1) of what was essential, as well as pleasurable, in a largely peasant lifestyle – the natural world around, human company, the reproduction of human life, as well as, inevitably, fighting and drinking. It is notable how rare religiosity and God feature in these most popular categories. At any rate, what is clear is that allusions made about love and marriage, while tending to be pessimistic or cynical, were also reasonably abundant in popular discourse.

Table 7.2 *Top ten topics, by number of entries, covered by Irish proverbs, as cited by O'Farrell (1980)*

Proverb classification	Number of entries
Nature (Animals)	34
Woman	34
Advice	33
Talk	33
Work	33
Marriage	31
Love	29
Family	27
Fighting	26
Alcohol	25

More broadly, if we want to get a sense of Ireland's interest in love, via a numerical analysis of her proverbs, we must be aware of the difference between social reality and physical reality. As the social psychologist Leon Festinger pointed out, we can directly test physical reality (Is a door locked? Try the handle and see) but social reality is always relative (We're rich only in so far as our neighbours are poor). Similarly, the degree to which Irish proverbs about love are central or trivial to Irish discourse partly depends on contrasting Ireland with other societies in this regard. The *Concise Oxford English Dictionary of Proverbs* (Simpson and Speake, 1993) provides a comparative British compilation of folk wisdom. It uses 327 different categorisations and includes 1,847 proverbs (although because of multiple entry under different categorisations, there are fewer than 1,847 separate proverbs included). Those that deal directly with love amount to only 29 proverbs (or 1.5 per cent) but other categories include attraction, beauty, marriage, weddings and, most loosely, friendship. The proverbs related to all of these together add to 62, or over three per cent of the total. In Table 7.3, the top ten categories, in terms of numbers of proverbs, are presented.

As can be seen by comparing Table 7.3 with either Tables 7.1 or 7.2, love appears to play as strong a role in the British tradition as the Irish. However, the increased priority given to 'money' and 'work' as well as a value like 'prudence' may reflect the response of popular idioms to earlier and more thoroughgoing industrialisation.

Finally, in Table 7.4, a summary of proverbs across the major languages of Europe (English, French, German, Italian, Spanish and Russian) is presented. These were collected in 1971 and the editor classified the proverbs into 48 different categories with a total of 1,101 proverbs. The category 'love and beauty' consists of 28 proverbs or 2.5 per cent roughly. As Table 7.4 shows, love is not included in a European-wide top ten. Thus it is certainly not *relatively* neglected as a topic in Irish proverbs and it plays at least as great a part in Irish sayings as elsewhere.

THE WISDOM OF PROVERBS?

If Ireland has in the past, and still does to an extent, relied on proverbs as a source of 'wisdom', one feels obliged then to ask, exactly how *wise* these sayings or proverbs are. For example, do they include, even in a contradictory way, some profound or insightful comments about the human condition generally, or about love and human relationships specifically? As rational individuals, we tend to rely on scientific research (or at least we like the idea that we do), to inform ourselves about important issues. What kind of things can we learn from the social psychological tradition of research into inter-personal attraction and close relationships? First, we discover that often we are somewhat unaware of what attracts us to others – people (especially men, but also women to a degree) underestimate how

Table 7.3 *Top ten topics, by number of entries, covered by British proverbs, as cited in the Concise Oxford Dictionary of Proverbs (1993)*

Proverb classification	Number of entries
Love	29
Money	25
Prudence	25
Size (Value of small and large things)	24
Work	24
Consequences (of actions)	23
Human nature	23
Patience	23
Weather	20
Good versus evil	19

Table 7.4 *Top ten topics, by number of entries, covered by cross-European proverbs (Gluski, 1971)*

Proverb classification	Number of entries
Ethics	41
Consequences (of actions)	37
Certainty-uncertainty	37
Uselessness	34
Money	33
Words related to deeds	33
Foolishness	30
Beginnings and ends	30
Weather	30
Consumption	30

much they are influenced simply by the physical good looks of others, rather than their personalities or other features we say we are interested in. We are also attracted, other things being equal, by familiarity with people and their appearances – more frequent interaction, and thus familiarity, increases in a surprisingly consistent way our attraction to others. We are also biased to believe that beauty tends to correlate or overlap with moral goodness. And we tend to prefer not just familiarity but also similarity – and to have more frequent and more rewarding relationships with people who share our views, and indeed prejudices.

We are also surprisingly accurate at selecting partners who have the same assets (looks, skills, talents, money, status) as ourselves. Indeed, many psychologists have suggested that relationships can be modelled in precisely the same way as virtually every other human behaviour, that is, as a fairly rational quasi-economic decision, for example we stick with our partner so long as the costs of leaving them are perceived to be higher than the benefits of staying with them. Within long-term relationships, consistent differences between men and women do emerge: men feel that women are too possessive; women feel that men are neglectful. Women are usually more aware that a relationship is in trouble and will use criticism to try to identify these problems and convey them to the man – many males simply withdraw or alternatively respond aggressively when these problems are outlined to them. They perceive problem-raising as a form of nagging. Persistent problems include a failure to see the world from the other's point of view, defensiveness, and an inability to provide positive feedback to the other about their abilities and skills. Biases include assuming the worst of why your partner did something rather than looking for benign interpretations of their action.

So, to what degree did proverbs educate the great mass of people by providing smart insights into the issue of attraction? To a reasonable one in fact. Modern social psychology distinguishes between two forms of romantic love: a passionate, head-over-heels type versus a companionate, shared-interest type. The former is a sharp flame, burning white and quickly, the latter a cosy fire. Researchers have found that for short-term relationships to evolve into satisfying long-term ones, they must survive the transition from the initial passionate infatuated type of love, usually expressed physically, to the comfortable shared warmth of companionate love, the actual appreciation of familiarity. But actually, this distinction is well recognised and represented in Irish proverbs, even if, as usual, it is given a pessimistic edge, i.e., recognising only the demise of passionate love, not its evolution. So we find such proverbs as 'love cools quickly' or 'wiggy (light) turf burns bright but not for long' (O'Farrell, 1980, p. 58). In fact, the proverb 'A flicker that burns is better than a blaze that burns', is an almost perfect summary of the dichotomy between passion and companionship (O'Farrell, 1980, p. 58).

Other psychologists have been interested in the area of biases – the pervasive misunderstandings and misperceptions of the world that people have. Within the area of interpersonal attraction, there is some convincing research about the failure of those in early stages of infatuation to make rational assessments of their new relationship. People also find it hard to see faults in their loved one that others can clearly identify. Buunk and van der Eijnden (1997) have found that early-stage couples tend to rate their relationships on average as better than others and often claim their love is unique. It also makes them uniquely bad at predicting how long a relationship will last and their close friends or housemates will generally provide much more accurate estimates of the likely longevity of the relationship (MacDonald and Ross, 1999). Thus the cynic at a wedding of a couple that have rushed into marriage who says, 'I'll give them six months' is often quite accurate. The reason for this misperception is actually quite rational. Early on in a relationship, people try to present an idealised version of themselves and conceal their flaws. Eventually, the truth will out of course. These biases are again summarised quite accurately in many Irish proverbs – for example, 'Love is blind but the neighbours see through it' (O'Farrell, 1980, p. 57) – has a modern ring. Similarly, we also find proverbs like 'love is not an impartial judge', or 'every thrush thinks her mate sings the sweetest' (touching on both the issues of biases and familiarity) (O'Farrell, 1980, pp. 57, 58). Most descriptively, if least poetically, about this phenomenon is the proverb, 'If a man is in love, he is no judge of beauty but when love wears off, he'll tell a woman about her warts' (O'Farrell, 1980, p. 58).

Other rediscovered aspects of the nature of attraction can be found in proverbs. Proverbs tend to recognise that older people can still enjoy the passion of love ('old coals are easiest kindled', O'Farrell, 1980, p. 57), unlike much of modern thinking which writes off their emotions or feelings. And recent feminist-inspired research has argued that women are still more likely to be successful in mating strategy if they play the conformist, agreeable, non-confrontational role. This inverse of this phenomenon is recognised in the proverb, 'If she has a mind of her own, there won't be many with a mind for her' (O'Farrell, 1980, p. 57). And the now accepted truism (accepted by most and certainly confirmed by psychological research) that couples have to inject their relationship with new ideas and 'constantly work at it' is also recognised in an old proverb – 'Love is like stirabout – it must be made fresh every day' (from O'Farrell, 1980, p. 57).

MISSING THE POINT? PROVERBS AND THE FUTURE OF LOVE

But there are certain aspects of love that simply are not recognised in proverbs. Their apparent pessimism has already been noted. They also have a one-sidedness, that more than borders on sexism. For example, far more of them deal with women than with men. In fact, they seem to be designed to speak to, or advise men about women, and often recommend why men should be cautious about women. This may not be such a bad thing, as a type of down-to-earth pre-marriage guidance, especially where none existed formally. However, it might have been more even-handed had women been also forewarned, but then they may not have had a great deal of choice in their partner. Proverbs also fail to reflect the current reality that the workplace is, for many people, the context where they met their partners or mates. Inevitably in an Ireland of the past, with heavy informal or indeed formal sexual segregation of most places of work, that simply was not a reality in people's lives. Likewise, the very idea of modern romance, and of a courtship pattern modelled on the North American pattern of dating – with ever deeper enmeshing of lives until a decision has to be made about whether house keys are to be shared – is entirely alien to the world from where proverbs came. In that world, marriages had at the very least a semi-arranged aspect, and courtship, if it existed at all, was probably, by modern standards, fairly 'short, nasty and brutish'.

Researchers today have begun to look at how the use of e-mail and phone-texting will alter patterns of communication in general and, along with web-dating, transform human relationships. Is it conceivable that proverbs, composed in a different age, and used by people who would find our lives even more bizarre and strange than we find theirs, will continue into the future to be relied upon? Before we reject the idea, it is worth remembering that the Bible was written from a culture which is vastly different from our own and yet millions of Christians claim to find it of continuing great relevance to their lives. Can proverbs about love remain valid in the future? Earlier in the chapter, we proposed that they are too cynical ('Love at first sight often happens in the twilight' – O'Farrell, 1980, p. 57; or 'A young man is bothered till he's married: after that he's bothered entirely' – Gaffney and Cashman, 1974, p. 67), too steeped in rural poverty ('If you love her in giobals [rags], your love will last' – O'Farrell, 1980)

Every thrush thinks her mate sings the sweetest. Dancing on the pier at Clogher, County Louth (1935).

or too grimly humorous ('Never make a toil of pleasure, as the man said when he dug his wife's grave only three feet deep' – Gaffney and Cashman, 1974). More *Desperate Housewives* perhaps than *Sex and the City*!

Yet many of us continue to believe that there *is* a wisdom in proverbs. But for this to be true, one must make a distinction between the outer form and kernel of inner truth of a saying. The former may be dated while the latter still resonates with a profound, if simple, truth. An analogy might be made with regard to homosexual relationships. Currently, there is a debate and controversy in some European countries, as well as US states, about whether legislation permitting civil union or perhaps marriages between same-sex couples should be introduced, and it seems likely that over time this will come to pass. It also seems likely that most of those using proverbs in the past considered them in terms of a married heterosexual relationship. But there is no reason to believe that proverbs capturing the essence of human affiliation will not provide just as adequate truths about same-sex relationships as more conventional ones. For example, 'Níl aon tseanstoca ná faigheann seanbhróg' ('There is never an old brogue but there is a foot to fit it' – Williams, 1992, p. 120) – is a simple statement of the pervasiveness of complementarity in relationships (which, incidentally, is another facet of interpersonal relations heavily researched by contemporary social psychologists). It was doubtlessly used in the past for the most part with heterosexuals in mind but its validity in other types of relationships will be proven over the changing times to come.

Mentioned earlier in this chapter was the idea expressed by some psychologists that love could be understood as simply another transaction, comparable to most economic phenomena. This is often known formally as equity theory. The key to economics is that it studies the allocation of scarce resources: by their very definition, people who are highly attractive are scarce in the general population ('attractiveness' in this context includes physical attractiveness but also other factors that contribute to a person's 'value' – intelligence, humour, personality, irritability, health as well as other factors such as their wealth and possessions). This sounds a rather cold and calculating way to think of love – but although it *is* calculating, it is rarely cold. The fact is that the pursuit of love is a powerful drive for most people and it would be bizarre if they did not invest the same energy and mental resources to this as to other goals in life. We may, with this perspective, begin to think of proverbs, especially the apparently cynical ones, as grittily honest about human nature, and about how tough, competitive and, yes, calculating people are when they pursue someone.

And yet proverbs duck the really tough part of relationships – breaking up. None of the Irish proverbs deals with splitting up or divorce, because of course such a course of action in a devout and religious people was virtually unknown. Instead, proverbs bluntly make clear the consequences of a rash decision: 'Marry in haste, repent at leisure' or 'Marriage changes a man and makes the woman that changed him whine about him not being the same man she married at all' (both from O'Farrell, 1980, p. 61). In their bluntness though, they may have provided those otherwise racing for marriage with something to ponder. And given the crisis in contemporary marriage, with ever-higher divorce rates in most Western countries, it may be that our unhealthy idealisation of love could benefit from some of the brutal realism of Irish proverbs. The American sociologist Norval Glenn (1991) examined opinion poll data on marriages beginning in the early 1970s in the USA. Aside from those ending in divorce, many married couples by the 1980s did not report themselves as 'very happy' in their relationship. He estimated that only about a quarter of marriages of the sample he examined could be described as successful, in that they contributed to the happiness of the people involved. An older set of proverbs warned people not to race into a relationship that the norms of the time meant was lifelong (like it or not). These proverbs need to be re-issued, re-used or re-invented for a new generation to warn them not to race into a relationship that may not turn out as they expect . . . 'Most Irishmen have the same wife for life, but she's not same woman' (O'Farrell, 1980, p. 63).

8

Poking Fun and Drawing Comparisons: Triadic Proverbs

'Half the wit and point of a proverb consists in its apt
application and the Irish, as might be expected, are
often peculiarly happy in this ...'
(MacAdam, cited in Williams, 1995, p. 346)

'Three with the best sight: the eye of a blacksmith on a
nail, the eye of a young girl at a contest, and the eye of
a priest on his parish'

INTRODUCTION

It has been said that there are two types of people – those who *believe*
that there are two types of people and those who do not (or who know
better). Whether or not one accepts this old witticism (commonly
attributed to P. G. Wodehouse), it is undeniable that typologies are
widely used in everyday life. Indeed, the process of assigning things
to mental categories or 'concepts' on the basis of apparently shared
characteristics is one of most powerful and enduring ways in which
people make sense of their experience. This is true because the world
has so many different people, objects and events that we would be
overwhelmed cognitively if we had to treat each one of them as
distinct or unique. Therefore, mental categories are essential tools in
our quest to simplify our experience. For example, in the wake of the
'9/11' terrorist atrocity, US President George W. Bush explicitly
divided the world into those who were 'with us' and those who were

'against us' – thereby revealing a form of 'tribal thinking' (Berreby, 2006) that is founded on simple, explicit categories. Many of the categories that we use in everyday life are *implicit*, however. For example, most of us distinguish between 'friends' (or people whom we trust and with whom we share certain personal information) and 'acquaintances' (or people to whom we may be friendly but to whom we generally avoid self-disclosure) although we probably could not explain precisely how someone qualifies for one or other of these categories. By the way, there is a long tradition of denigrating people who occupy 'out-group' categories. Thus, as we explained in chapter 1, Roback's (1944) *Dictionary of International Slurs* reveals how people tend to make disparaging rather than flattering allusions to people who are not of their own 'kind' (Raymond, 1956).

Not surprisingly, mental categories serve as the building blocks of our thinking. This happens because the very act of classifying something encourages us to think about what that thing has in common with other members of the category to which it has been assigned. To illustrate, if you were buying a birthday present for a relative's child, you might try to find out what sort of gift a *typical* child of that age would enjoy. In this way, mental categories force us to think abstractly. Categorisation is also used extensively in humour. For example, Dubliners from the 'southside' and the 'northside' have poked fun at each other for centuries – as do people from different nationalities and rival ethnic groups. Of course, an unfortunate by-product of such classification is that it can lead to stereotyping and prejudice. These problems tend to occur whenever we respond to people *solely* in terms of the categories to which we have assigned them (for example, 'immigrants') rather than as unique individuals.

Given the central role of categorisation in human thinking, it is not surprising that certain Irish sayings rely on classifications to transmit their messages. And so, the present chapter explores a set of Irish proverbs called 'triads' which use tripartite classifications to comment on, satirise and/or convey insights into various everyday topics. As we shall see, although many of these trichotomies are provocative in appearing to perpetuate certain stereotypes, others challenge them in subtle, ironic ways. To illustrate the former, consider the 'three things that are the giddiest: a young widow, a kitten and a kid goat' ('An trí is mó giodam: Baintreach óg mná, piscín cait agus mionnán gabhair'). Here, the caricature of the merry young widow is conveyed through comparison with the flighty behaviour of immature animals. However, triads sometimes challenge popular opinion. For example, in Kuno Meyer's (1906) collection of Irish triads obtained mainly from the fourteenth to the nineteenth centuries, we learn that there are 'three silences that are better than speech: Silence during instruction, silence during music and silence during preaching'. This veneration of certain kinds of silence is interesting because it challenges the stereotypical belief that Irish people are garrulous. Other (non-triadic) proverbs highlight the virtue of silence more poetically. For example, the expression 'a silent mouth is sweet-sounding' ('binn béal ina thost'; Partridge, 1978, p. 4) is often quoted when someone evokes anger in another person by saying too much or by engaging in verbal rudeness. Similarly, the dangerous consequences of a loose tongue are indicated by the Irish expression 'A person's mouth often broke his own nose' ('Is minic a bhris béal duine a shrón'). Other proverbs emphasise the importance of maintaining a tactful silence when necessary: 'A wise head makes a closed mouth' ('Deineann ceann ciallmhar béal iadta') and 'When wrathful words arise, a closed mouth is soothing' ('Air teacht na bhfocal borb is binn béal iadta').

In this chapter, we shall explore the origin, structure and psychological significance of triadic proverbs. Specifically, we tackle three main questions. Firstly, what are 'triads', where do they come from and how are they organised? Secondly, what is the significance of the tendency to group things in threes? Finally, and perhaps most importantly, what can we learn from triads about the topics and experiences to which they refer?

WHAT ARE TRIADS? NATURE, ORIGIN AND STRUCTURE

Triads are aphoristic, figurative expressions which display a distinctive structure. Typically, they begin with a line that describes a category (such as the 'three sharpest things imaginable' or the 'three most sensitive parts of one's body'). Then, they provide some relevant details of, or comments on, certain members of that category. Finally, the punchline is supplied in the form of a witty, ironic and/or scatological remark. Usually, this final line is memorable because it violates the expectations created by the initial statement. For example, there are 'three smiles that are worse than sorrow: The smile of snow as it melts, the smile of your wife on you after another man has been with her, the grin of a hound ready to leap at you' (Appletree Press, 1996, p. 21). A variation of this expression proposes that the 'three worst smiles are the smile of a wave, the smile of a foolish woman, and the smile of a hound about to leap' ('Trí luchra atá measa: luchra tuinde, luchra mná bóithe, luchra con fóleimnige'). Clearly, the idea conveyed here is that smiling can often conceal treachery. In other words, the usual meaning of a smile is subverted by its association with unpleasant emotions such as loss, deception and threat. Not all triads end with a punchline, however. Consider 'three disagreeable things at home: a scolding wife, a smoking chimney and a leaky roof' ('Na trí nithe is measa i dtig – báirseach mná, simné deataig agus an díon a bheith ag leigean tríd'). An unusual feature of this proverb is that the key phrase ('a scolding wife') appears at the *beginning* rather than at the end of the triad.

Although the precise origins of triads are somewhat obscure, most scholars agree that they probably date back at least as far as the ninth century. At that time, a document called the 'Trecheng Breth Féne' or Triad of Judgements, was issued and it contained over 200 examples of proverbial expressions presented in triadic form. It is possible that triadic expressions existed in Irish before the ninth century, however. Thus the 'Cambray Homily' (a document from the seventh century which is one of the oldest surviving examples of written Irish) suggested that there were are 'three kinds of martyrdom' (Fios Feasa, 1998).

Technically, triads are part of a larger family of enumerative proverbs which seek to link together, or comment on, a stated number of phenomena (Williams, 1988). This family includes 'duads' (for example, 'two things you will not fret at if you are a wise man: the thing you can't help and the thing you can'), 'tetrads' (for example, 'Ceathrar sagart gan a bheith santach, ceathrar gaibhne gan a bheith buí, ceathrar seanbhan gan a bheith mantach: Sin dáréag nach bhfuil sa tír' – 'Four priests who are not greedy, four blacksmiths who are not dark-skinned, four old women who are not gap-toothed: those are twelve who are not in the country'; Fios Feasa, 1998) and a even a 'heptad' ('seven prohibitions: to go security for an outlaw, for a jester and for a madman, for a person without bonds, for an unfilial person, for an imbecile, for one excommunicated'; Meyer, 1906, p. 235). In passing, it is notable that the number 'seven' is also significant in the oral folk tradition. There are seven deadly sins, seven seas, seven wonders of the world, seven notes in the Western musical scale and apparently, 'seven habits of highly successful people' (as proposed by Stephen Covey (1989) in a book which has sold over 15 million copies). Perhaps not surprisingly, an 'eighth habit' of successful people has recently been promulgated by Covey in the quest to move from effectiveness to 'greatness'.

Triads are different from other enumerative proverbs, however, because instead of referring to different 'kinds' of things, triads typically indicate different *features* of the same thing. For example, in exploring expertise in music, we learn that there are 'three things that constitute a harper: a tune to make you cry, a tune to make you laugh, and a tune to put you to sleep'. In a similar vein, there are three 'things that cannot be done: whistle and chew meal, make a stick without two ends on it, get two bills without a hollow between them'. Here, three things with a common feature (in this case, impossible

actions) are classified together. Alternatively, the three most important features of a given phenomenon are specified. For example,
'a good surgeon must have – an eagle's eye, a lady's hand, and a
lion's heart' (Williams, 1988, p. 60).

Part of the appeal of triads is that their classifications are rarely
neutral. Instead, they tend to convey a vitriolic message by providing
an ironic, satirical or cynical commentary on a topic. For example,
consider 'Three things bright at first, then dull and finally black:
co-operation, a marriage alliance and living in the one house'. This
proverb conveys the rather cynical idea that people find it difficult to
work or live with each other. Another triad postulates 'the three
sharpest things on earth: A hen's eye after a grain, a blacksmith's eye
after a nail, and an old woman's eye after her son's wife' ('Na trí nithe
is géire are bith: Súil circe in ndiaidh gráinne, súil gabha in ndiaidh
tairne, agus súil caillí in ndiaidh bean a mic'). Here, the visual acuity
of a mother-in-law is highlighted by comparing it with the vigilance
of hen or a blacksmith in their daily work. Happily, a less cynical
version of this triad exists in which 'the eye of a man after his true
love' (or 'súil an fhir i ndiaidh a ghrá ghil') replaces the scrutiny of a
mother-in-law. In general, however, the juxtapositions and punch-
lines found in triadic proverbs are acerbic in nature.

Having discussed the nature and structure of triads, let us now
consider some possible explanations for the tripartite distinctions
that they provide. In short, what is special about the number three
in this type of proverb?

THE SIGNIFICANCE OF THE NUMBER
THREE IN ANCIENT IRELAND

The number three has long held a special significance in Western
culture – perhaps because of our tripartite tense system (Dundes,
1981). To illustrate, trifold repetition is ubiquitous in puzzles (for

example, the riddle of the Sphinx explores the three ages of the person), jokes (such as those with three principals – an Englishman, a Scotsman and an Irishman), folk speech (for example, one gives three cheers for someone) and political slogans ('liberté, égalité, fraternité'). 'Threeness' was also venerated by the ancient Irish. For example, legend suggests that the Fianna were celebrated for three unique virtues – purity of heart, strength of limb and acting in accordance with their word. A similar reverence for the number three may explain why some Irish wakes (see also chapter 6) lasted for three days and three nights. More generally, this number is associated with a host of superstitions around the world (Roud, 2003). For example, odd numbers are generally seen as lucky whereas even numbers are perceived as unfortunate. Indeed, Shakespeare accepted this point when a character in *The Merry Wives of Windsor* says 'no more prattling, go; I'll hold. This is the third time. I hope good luck lies in odd numbers . . . They say there is divinity in odd numbers'.

Research on numerology confirms the special status of the number three in many cultures (MacKillop, 2001). For example, the Greek philosopher Pythagoras regarded it as the perfect number because it has connotations of the different dimensions of time – past, present and future. Endorsing such beliefs, the ancient Irish people also attached a special importance to this number ('the favourite number of early Ireland'; MacKillop, 2001, p. 113). Celtic society distinguished between three types of people – priests, warriors and agriculturalists (Curran, 1999) and representations of three-headed gods and goddesses have been found in many ancient Irish sites such as the famous three-faced stone head found in Corleck, County Cavan which dates back to the Celtic Iron Age. Symbolically, the three faces could simultaneously look at the past, present and future (Ó hÓgáin, 2002). In a similar vein, the largest passage-grave discovered at Newgrange displays three interlocking spirals. Likewise, Celtic mythology suggests that there were three female divine eponyms of ancient Ireland – Macha, Badb and Morrigain (Morrigu) (Curran, 1999). More generally, according to MacCana (1980), ancient Ireland was famous for representing its deities in triadic form. Furthermore, tripartite classifications were also evident in traditional Irish pipe music. Thus the bards distinguished between *golltraí* (slow airs), *geantraí* (dance music) and *suantraí* (lullabies). Ó hÓgáin (2002) also highlighted the significance of 'three' among the ancient Irish. Specifically, he claimed that 'this is a very old belief, for the early literature refers to several Celtic deities who were triplicate. Major events in folk stories often occur three times, and triadic expressions figure prominently in Irish proverbs. This number has connotations of roundness and totality, and many ritual acts, such as walking around a bonfire on St. John's Night or doing rounds at a holy well, were performed thrice. If one dreamed of the same thing on three nights running, this was taken as proof that the dream was true' (Ó hÓgáin, 2002, p. 112).

The number three also features in Irish folklore on the shamrock (a trifoliate plant also known as the trefoil) which is recognised around the world as the national symbol of Ireland and 'Irishness', perhaps even eclipsing the harp as the prototypical emblem of the country. Legend suggests that it was used by St Patrick in an attempt to explain the mystery of the Holy Trinity to the pagan Irish during the fifth century (Curran, 1999). One of the earliest written accounts of this alleged conversion came from Edward Jones (1794, cited in Roud, 2003) who reported that:

> When St Patrick landed near Wicklow the inhabitants were ready to stone him for attempting an innovation in the religion of their ancestors. He requested to be heard, and explained unto them that God is an omnipresent, sacred spirit, who created heaven and earth, and that the Trinity is contained in the Unity; but they were reluctant to give credit to his words. St Patrick, therefore, plucked a trefoil from the ground and expostulated with the Hibernians: 'Is it not as feasible for the Father,

Son, and Holy Ghost, as for these three leaves thus to grow upon a single stalk'. Then, the Irish were immediately convinced of their error, and were solemnly baptised by St Patrick' (Roud, 2003, p. 401).

Although this well-known story does not appear in earlier biographies of St Patrick, and is hence highly questionable (see also Forrestall, 1930), it became synonymous with him from the eighteenth century onwards.

Of course, cultural factors often shape the evolution of mental categories. For example, in the Australian Aboriginal language Dyirbal, a category called *balan* exists which juxtaposes three apparently unrelated phenomena – 'women, fire and dangerous things' (Lakoff, 1987). Obviously, this category was not formed by the conjunction of common features because *balan* also includes birds that are not dangerous as well as unusual animals like the platypus. How could it have evolved? One anthropological explanation is that it arose from the fact that in Aboriginal thought, the sun (a woman) is the wife of the moon and gives off heat. Therefore, it is associated with 'fire' and since fire is dangerous, women are linked with it. Unfortunately, this explanation is incomplete because the category *balan* also includes stars and some types of trees. Given such complications, perhaps the origin of this Aboriginal category will remain obscure

In summary, the distinctive structure of triads appears to have at least two different roots. On the one hand, as we have seen, there is a long folk tradition of grouping things in threes for reasons of good luck. Thus, in British and Irish superstitions, odd numbers are generally regarded as being luckier than even numbers (see 'third time lucky') – although there are exceptions such as the common belief that 'bad things come in threes'. On the other hand, it is possible that triads are derived mainly from Old Testament enumerative expressions (McCone, 1990). An example to support this theory may be found in the Book of Wisdom (Ecclesiasticus 25: 1) which proclaims that 'there are three things my soul delights in and which bare delightful to God – concord between brothers, friendship between neighbours and a wife and husband who live happily together'.

Regardless of their origins, triads are usually memorable for a simple reason. Briefly, their tripartite organisation reflects the approximate lower limit of our short-term or 'working' memory system. This system is known to psychologists as the 'desktop' of the mind because it serves as a virtual workspace when we are performing tasks which require us to put some information on hold in our minds while processing other information. For example, imagine listening to someone who is telling you some news using a long sentence. The news would be unintelligible if you did not have the ability to store the first part of the sentence in your mind temporarily while you processed the last part of the sentence. Likewise, the ability to remember people's names when you are being introduced to them requires working memory as does the ability to give and receive directions. Since the 1950s, research on the span of our working memory system has shown that people can recall only three to nine separate items unaided. Briefly, in a typical experiment, people would be given a variety of sequences of things (for example, numbers, colours, names) to recall in their correct order. Results showed that most people could remember only about seven items in any list in their correct order. This led psychologists to conclude that the span of immediate memory was somewhere between three and nine items, with an average of about seven separate items. In summary, triads may be memorable simply because they lie well within the limits of our fragile working memory span.

EXPLORING THE WISDOM OF TRIADS
THEMES AND COMMENTS

Given the diversity of topics covered by triads, it is difficult to provide a succinct yet representative summary of the insights which they yield. A flavour of such insights is apparent in the following summary, however.

Cynical views of women

Misogynistic comments are readily identifiable in many triadic classifications. We are told that there are 'three kinds of women: the woman as shameless as a pig, the woman as unruly as a hen, and the woman as gentle as a lamb' ('Na trí sagahas ban: bean chomh mí-náireach leis an muic, bean chomh crostáltha leis a gcirc, agus bean chomh mín leis an uan'). Venturing beyond such crude typologies, it is clear that many triads portray women as being talkative, incomprehensible, nasty to each other and obstinate. For example, consider the proposition that there are 'three things that never get rusty: a woman's tongue, the shoes of a butcher's horse, and the money of the charitable' ('Trí rud ná thagann aon mheirg orthu: teanga mná, cruite capaill búistéara, agus airgead lucht carthan-achta'). A similar claim that women love idle talk is evident in other (non-triadic) proverbs and sayings. The confluence of women, fire and gossip is apparent in the following figurative expression: 'Where there is heat, there are women and where there are women, there is gossip' ('An áit a mbíon teas bíonn mná agus an áit a mbíonn mná bíonn geab'). This emphasis on gossip is enshrined in another old saying which suggests that there are three ways of transmitting a message quickly – telegraph, telephone and tell a woman! Women are also portrayed as being unfathomable in many triadic proverbs. For example, we learn that there are 'three kinds of men who fail to understand women: young men, old men and middle-aged men'

143

(Gaffney and Cashman, 1974, p. 83). Clearly, the implication here is that *nobody* can understand women. This idea is repeated in another triad which claims that there are 'three things that Aristotle couldn't understand: the work of the bees, the ebb and flow of the tide, and the mind of a woman' ('Trí rud a chuaigh d'Arastaitíl: saothar na mbeach, teacht is imeacht na taoide, intinn na mban'). Another version of this proverb identifies 'The three most incomprehensible things in the world: the mind of a woman, the labour of the bees, and the ebb and flow of the tide' ('Na trí rud is deacra do thuiscint sa domhan – inntleacht na mban, obair na mbeach, teacht is imeacht na taoide'). Women were also portrayed as being irritating ('The three most bothersome things in the world: a thorn in the foot, a woman, and a goat going to the fair that will go any way but the way you want it') and unpleasant to each other ('Two cats and one mouse, two dogs and one bone, two women in one house will not agree long!'; Williams, 1988, p. 61). Obstinacy was also perceived as a feminine characteristic: 'Three things without rule: a woman, a mule and a pig' ('Triúr gan riaghal – ban, muile agus muc'). Given such views, it is hardly surprising that women were sometimes perceived as being ineducable: 'The three most difficult to teach: a mule, a pig, and a woman' (or alternatively, 'The three most difficult to teach: a woman, a scythe and a razor'). Strangely (even by the chauvinistic logic of the time!), women were also regarded as being a liability in the home: 'The three worst things to have in a house: a scolding wife, a smokey chimney and a leaky roof'. Indeed, the contrast between men and women in this regard is highlighted by the following triads: 'Three things that are best in a house: oxen, men and axes' and 'Three things that are worst in a house: boys, women, lewdness'. To make matters worse, women were expected to refrain from certain actions such as whistling! Thus there were 'three things Christ never intended: a woman whistling, a hound howling, and a hen crowing'. In passing, it is interesting to note that whistling is also associated with foolishness: 'The three

Trí rud ná thagann aon mheirg orthu: Teanga mná, cruite capaill búistéara agus airgead lucht carthanachta (Three things that never get rusty: A woman's tongue, the shoes of a butcher's horse, and the money of the charitable).
Women with shawls, An Ceathrú Rua, County Galway (1936).

signs of a fool: whistling, a tilted cap, and questions' ('Trí chom-hartha an amadáin: fead, feirc, is fiafraí').

Certain kinds of bad luck were also likely if one were female: 'The three ugliest things of their own kind: a thin red-haired woman, a thin yellow horse, and a thin white cow'. Similarly, it was said that the 'Three unluckiest things to meet first thing in the morning: a mad dog, a man who lent you money and a red-haired girl'. Interestingly, Roud (2003) noted that there has been a long history of distrust of red-haired people in Britain and Ireland. Traditionally, such people were seen as being devious, cruel, hot-tempered, untrustworthy and unlucky. This superstition was especially prevalent among fisher-men who would often return home if they encountered a red-haired woman when preparing to go to sea (Ó hÓgáin, 2002). Among the ancient Irish, hair colour was thought to reflect blood characteristics – hence red-haired people were regarded as being fiery tempered.

Despite such acerbic portraits of women, a minority of triads have some sympathy for them. For example, the hard life of married women was acknowledged in such expressions as: 'Three drops of a married woman: a drop of blood, a teardrop, a drop of sweat'. Likewise, there are 'three things a man should not be without: a cat, a chimney and a housewife'. Of course, by current standards, the sympathetic tone of the latter proverb could be regarded as extremely patronising.

Transience, heredity and ageing

A number of triads comment on the transience of life. For example, there are 'Three things that don't remain: a white cow, a handsome woman and a house on a height' ('Trí nithe nach buan – bó bhán, bean bhreágh, tigh ar árd'). Another version of this proverb claims that there 'Three things whose beauty does not last: a house on a hill, a white horse, a fine woman' ('Trí nithe nach gcoineann a slacht i bhfad: Teach ar árd, capall bán, bean bhreá'). Similarly, there are

146

'Three things that survive for the shortest time: a woman's association, the love of a mare for her foal, and fresh oaten bread'. An
alternative version of this latter proverb proposes that there are
'three things that leave the shortest traces: a bird on a branch, a ship
on the sea and a man on a woman'. By contrast, there are 'Three things
that remain longest in a family: fighting, red-hair and thieving'.

The importance of heredity is also a recurrent theme in many
triadic expressions. For example, it was commonly believed that
artistic abilities and certain personal qualities were innate: 'Three
things that cannot be acquired: a singing voice, generosity and
poetry' ('Trí ní nach féidir a mhúineadh: guth, féile, is filíocht'). In
addition, according to Ó hÓgáin (2002), there is a strong belief in
Irish folklore that wisdom could not be learned.

Curiously, many triads show scant respect for old age: 'the three
things useless when old: an old schoolmaster, an old horse and an old
soldier', and 'three things that don't bear nursing: an old woman, a
hen and a sheep'. Given this view, it is most surprising that there
were 'three to whom it's little sense to pay a compliment: an old man,
a bad man and a child'. Likewise, altruistic actions for certain people
were frowned upon: 'Three kind acts unrequited: that done for an
old man, for a wicked person or for a little child'. A somewhat
Darwinian explanation for this rather cynical view of the elderly
people was suggested by Williams (1988, p. 66), who observed that
people may have thought that those who were in the last stage of life
may not have time to repay favours. Similarly, a bad person would
not repay a favour anyway and a child would be too young to
understand or appreciate a charitable action. Little sympathy is
evident for loneliness among the elderly: 'Three things there is no
cure for: mist at the end of a moon, rain at the end of a day and mist
in an old person's eye'. At least one triad offers sympathy for the
elderly, however. Thus there are 'Three rude ones of the world: a
youngster mocking an old man, a healthy person mocking an invalid,
a wise man mocking a fool'.

Virtues and vices

Many triads convey disapproval of certain vices and breaches of social etiquette. For example, consider 'Three prohibitions of food: to eat it without giving thanks, to eat it before its proper time, to eat it after a guest'. The virtue of friendship is also indicated by expressions such as 'Three best things to have a surplus of: money after paying the rent, seed after spring and friends at home'. By contrast, the vice of meanness is highlighted by proverbs such as 'The three worst afflictions: miserliness of heart, narrowness of house and scantness of pot' ('An trí anacair is measa: cúngrach croí, cúngrach tí, cúngrach corcáin'). On the other hand, there are 'Three good things to have: a clean shirt, a clean conscience and a guinea in the pocket'. Breaches of social etiquette are also admonished by triads such as: 'The three worst departures: leaving Mass before it ends, leaving table without grace and leaving your wife to go to another woman'. Boastfulness was also regarded as being unacceptable socially. Thus there are 'Three things a man should not boast of: the size of his purse, the beauty of his wife and the sweetness of his beer'.

Poverty and misfortune

Good fortune is often associated with material possessions in triads. Thus 'The three most fortunate things a man ever had: a mare, a sow and a goose'. But there are different types of wealth: 'Three wealths in barren places: a well in a mountain, fire out of a stone, wealth in the possession of a mean man'. The last line of this proverb indicates that wealthy people may be emotionally impoverished if their meanness prevents them from enjoying the benefits of their riches. Not surprisingly, various types of poverty have also been identified. For example, one triad states that there are 'three kinds of poor people: the man poor by the will of God, the man poor by his own will, and the man poor even if he owned the world' ('Trí shaghas bocht:

Trí ní nach féidir a mhúineadh: Guth, féile, is filíocht (Three things that cannot be taught: a singing voice, generosity and poetry). Mummers, Carcur, County Wexford (1947).

duine bocht le toil Dé, duine bocht lena thoil féin, agus duine bocht dá mbeadh an saol aige').

Emotions and personal qualities

Some of the most evocative triads are those which describe emotions in terms of natural forces. For example, consider the suggestion regarding 'Three greatest rushes: the rush of water, the rush of fire and the rush of falsehood'. An alternative version of this triad proposes 'Three fastest runs: the run of fire, the run of water, and the run of a lie' ('An trí rith is mó: rith tine, rith uisce agus rith éithigh'). These triads convey a powerful image of lies spreading like a flood or like wildfire. Similarly, fire and water are powerful metaphors for emotions such as hatred: 'Three strongest forces: the force of fire, the force of water and the force of hatred'. Other emotions that are examined in triads include trust and danger. Thus there are 'Three things not to be trusted: a fine day in winter, the life of an old person or the word of an important man – unless it's in writing'. Again, this triad displays a rather cynical view of old age. With regard to dangerous things, anti-English sentiments are apparent in certain triads. For example, there are 'Three most dangerous things: the forehead of a bull, the back of a stallion and the laugh of an Englishman' ('Trí rud is dáinseara amuigh: éadan tairbh, deireadh staile, gáire an tSasanaigh'). Emotions are sometimes linked to illness in certain triads: 'Three diseases without shame: Love, itch, and thirst' (Trí ghalar gan náire: Grá, tochas, agus tart'). By contrast, emotions such as contentment are also covered in triads like 'The three sweetest sounds there are: the bellowing of a cow, the grinding of a millstone, the screaming of a child'. Although these latter sounds are initially irritating, they may be interpreted as reflections of an enviable prosperity. Finally, emotions like love are portrayed as being powerful yet invisible: 'Three things that cannot be seen: an edge, the wind and love' ('Trí ní nach feidir a fheiscint: faobhar, gaoth agus grá').

Characteristics of animals

Domestic and wild animals feature in many Irish triads. Usually, certain traits or sensory skills are attributed to them. Among farm animals, bulls were especially valued for their strength: 'Three traits of a bull: a bold walk, a strong neck and a hard forehead'. Foxes, cats and hares are also prominent: 'Three gifts of the fox: A sharp eye, a careful ear, a bushy tail' ('Trí bhua an tsionnaigh: Súil bhiorach, cluas aireach, eiraball scothach'). Similarly, 'Three traits of a fox: a light step, a look to the front and a glance at each side of the road'. Cats were believed to have certain supernatural qualities because they are night hunters: 'Three gifts of the cat: sight in the dark, walking without noise, a woman's mistake' ('Trí bhua an chait: léargas sa dhorchadas, siúl gan torann, dearmad bhean an tí'. The most obvious feature of a hare was its speed: 'Three traits of a hare: a lively ear, a bright eye and a quick run against the hill' or 'Three skills of the hare: sharp turning, high jumping and strong running against the hill'. Interestingly, hares have long been regarded as unlucky, if not sinister, creatures in ancient Ireland (Ó hÓgáin, 2002). Finally, a warning is evident about 'The three worst pets: a pet priest, a pet beggar and a pet pig'. The anti-clerical sentiments expressed here are somewhat unusual in triads.

In this chapter, we explained that classification, or the process of assigning things to mental categories according to a given rule, helps people to make sense of their experience and to take appropriate actions accordingly. This process of grouping things together lies at the heart of a set of enumerative Irish proverbs called triads which use tripartite classifications (trichotomies) of things in order to comment on, and provided insights into, various everyday topics. Remarkably, some triadic proverbs are over a thousand years old. Having considered the structure of triads, we examined the significance of the number 'three' in ancient Ireland from the perspective of folklore, mythology and psychology. In the final section of the chapter, we explored some key themes and insights which emerge from an analysis of a variety of triads. From our analysis, it is clear that although many of these expressions are somewhat cynical and anachronistic, they can occasionally yield insights that are fresh, challenging and timeless.

References

Akenson, D. (2005). *An Irish History of Civilization*, vol. 1. New York: Granta.

Andreasen, N. C, (1977). 'Reliability and validity of proverb interpretation to assess mental status', *Comprehensive Psychiatry*, *18*, pp. 465–72.

Appletree Press (1996). *The Pick of Irish Wisdom*. Belfast: Appletree Press.

Arora, S. L. (1984). 'The perception of proverbiality', *Proverbium*, *1*, pp. 1–38.

Asch (1946). 'Forming impressions of personality', *Journal of Abnormal and Social Psychology*, *41*, pp. 258–90.

Barnes-Holmes, D., Cochrane, A., Barnes-Holmes, Y., and Stewart, I. (2004). '"Offer it up" and psychological acceptance: Empirical evidence for your grandmother's wisdom', *The Irish Psychologist*, *31*, 72–9.

Benjamin, J. (1944). 'A method for distinguishing and evaluating formal thinking disorders in schizophrenia', in J. Kasamin (ed.), *Language and Thought in Schizophrenia* (pp. 65–90). Berkeley: University of California Press.

Berkowitz, L. (1972). 'Frustrations, comparisons, and other sources of emotion aroused as contributors to social unrest', *Journal of Social Issues*, 28, pp. 77–92.

Bernstein, D. A., Penner, L. A., Clarke-Stewart, A. and Roy, E. J. (2003). *Psychology*, 6th edn. Boston: Houghton Mifflin.

Berreby, D. (2006). *Us and Them: Understanding Your Tribal Mind.* London: Hutchinson.

Birnbaum, N. J. (1971). *Towards a Critical Sociology*. Oxford: Oxford University Press.

Brickman, P. and Campbell, D. T. (1971). 'Hedonic relativism and planning the good society', in M. H. Appley (ed.), *Adaptation-Level Theory* (pp. 287–305). New York: Academic Press.

Buunk, B. P., and van der Eijnden, R. J. (1997). 'Perceived prevalence, perceived superiority, and relationship satisfaction: Most relationships are good, but ours is the best', *Personality and Social Psychology Bulletin*, *23*, pp. 219–28.

Carr, P. (1991). *The Big Wind: The Story of the Legendary Big Wind of 1839, Ireland's Greatest Natural Disaster*. Belfast: White Row Press.

Cash, T. F., and Derlega, V. J. (1978). 'The matching hypothesis: Physical attractiveness among same-sexed friends', *Personality and Social Psychology Bulletin*, *4*, pp. 240–3.

Connolly, S. J. (ed.) (1998). *Oxford Companion to Irish History*. Oxford: Oxford University Press.

Covey, Stephen (1989). *The Seven Habits of Highly Effective People*. New York: Simon & Schuster.

Cummings, J. (1985). *Clinical Neuropsychology*. Orlando, Florida: Grune & Stratton.

Curran, B. (1999). *The Wolfhound Guide to the Shamrock*. Dublin: Wolfhound.

Dolan, T. P. (2004). *A Dictionary of Hiberno-English: The Irish Use of English*. Dublin: Gill & Macmillan.

Dorson, R. (1972). *Folklore and Folklife: An Introduction*. Chicago: University of Chicago Press.

Dundes, A. (1981). 'On the structure of the proverb', in W. Mieder and A. Dundes (eds), *The Wisdom of Many: Essays on the Proverb* (pp. 43–64). New York: Garland.

Dundes, A. (1984). 'On whether weather proverbs are proverbs', *Proverbium*, *1*, pp. 39–46.

Edwards, T. B. (2004). *Irish: A Dictionary of Phrases, Terms and Epithets Beginning With The Word 'Irish'*, Cork: Mercier.

Epstein, R. (1997). 'Folk wisdom: Was your grandmother right?', *Psychology Today*, November/December, pp. 1–27.

Eret, D. C. (2001). 'The past does not equal the future: Anthony Robbins' self-help maxims as therapeutic forms of proverbial rhetoric', *Proverbium*, *18*, pp. 77–103.

Fergusson, R. (ed.) (1983). *The Penguin Dictionary of Proverbs*. London: Penguin.

Fios Feasa (1998). *Irish Proverbs: Sayings, Blessings, Curses etc.* (CD). Kerry: Fios Feasa.

Fitzgerald, C. (2004). *The Weather is a Good Storyteller*. Dublin: Ashfield Press.

Fitzgerald, P. (2003). 'American wake', in B. Lalor (ed.), *The Encyclopaedia of Ireland* (p. 22). Dublin: Gill & Macmillan.

Flanagan, L. (1995). *Irish Proverbs*. Dublin: Gill & Macmillan.

Forrestall, J. (1930). 'The shamrock tradition', *Irish Ecclesiastical Record*, *36*, pp. 63–74.

Foster , R. F. (2001), *The Irish Story: Telling Tales and Making It Up in Ireland*. London: Allen Lane.

Furnham, A. F. (1987). 'The proverbial truth: Contextually reconciling the truthfulness of antonymous proverbs', *Journal of Language and Social Psychology*, *6*, pp. 49–59.

Gaffney, S., and Cashman, S. (1974). *Proverbs and Sayings of Ireland*. Dublin: Wolfhound.

Galbraith, J. K. (1969). *The Affluent Society* (2nd edn). London: Hamish Hamilton.

Gershaw, D. A. (1999). 'I knew it all along', www.members.cox.net/dangershaw/lol/HindsightBias.html

Gibbs, R. W., and Beitel, D. (1995). 'What proverb understanding reveals about how people think', *Psychological Bulletin*, *118*, 133–54.

Giles, B. (1990). *The Story of Weather*. London: Her Majesty's Stationery Office in association with Shell UK.

Glenn, N. D. (1991). 'The recent trend in marital success in the United States', *Journal of Marriage and the Family*, *53*, pp. 261–70.

Gluski, J. (1971). *Proverbs: A Comparative Book of English, French, German, Italian, Spanish and Russian Proverbs*. Amsterdam: Elsevier.

Gorham, D. R. (1956). 'A proverbs test for clinical and experimental use', *Psychological Reports*, *1*, pp. 1–12.

Haidt, J. (2006). *The Happiness Hypothesis: Finding Modern Truths in Ancient Wisdom*. New York: Basic Books.

Hayden, T. (2001). *Irish on the Inside: In Search of the Soul of Irish America*. London: Verso.

Hernardi, P. and Steen, F. (1999). 'The topical landscapes of proverbial: A cross-disciplinary travelogue', *Style*, *33*, pp. 1–20.

Hickey, T. (2005). Personal communication (16 December).

Hobsbawm, E. J. (1994). *Age of Extremes: The Short Twentieth Century, 1914–1991*. London: Michael Joseph.

Hogg, M. and Vaughan, G. (2002). *Social Psychology*, 3rd edn. London: Prentice Hall.

Holland, T. (2003). *Rubicon: The Triumph and Tragedy of the Roman Republic*. London: Little Brown.

Hughes, A. J. (1998). *Robert Shipboy MacAdam: His Life and Gaelic Proverb Collection*. Belfast: Institute of Irish Studies, Queen's University.

Huntingdon, S. P. (1968). *Political Order in Changing Societies*, New Haven: Yale University Press.

Jacobs, J. (1899). 'The dying of death', *Fortnightly Review*, New Series 72, 264–9.

Joyce, J. (1960 [1922]). *Ulysses*. London: Bodley Head.

Kelly, F. (1996). *The Pick of Irish Wisdom: An Illustrated Selection of Irish Triads*. Dublin: Appletree.

Keneally, Thomas (1972). *The Chant of Jimmie Blacksmith*. Sydney and London: Angus Robertson.

Kiberd, D. (1989). 'Irish literature and Irish history' in R. Foster (ed.), *The Oxford Illustrated History of Ireland* (pp. 275–337). Oxford: Oxford University Press.

Kiberd, D. (1993). *Synge and the Irish Language* (2nd ed.). Houndmills, Basingstoke: Macmillan.

Kingsbury, S. A., Kingsbury, M. E., and Mieder, W. (1996). *Weather Wisdom: Proverbs, Superstitions and Signs*. New York: Peter Lang.

Kirshenblatt-Gimblett, B. (1981). 'Toward a theory of proverb meaning', in W. Mieder and A. Dundes (eds), *The Wisdom of Many: Essays on the Proverb* (pp. 111–21). New York: Garland.

Knauth, P. (1996). 'Designing better shift systems', *Applied Ergonomics*, 27, pp. 39–44.

Knowles, E. (1997). *The Oxford Dictionary of Phrase, Saying and Quotation*. Oxford: Oxford University Press.

Lakoff, G. (1987). *Women, Fire and Dangerous Things*. Chicago: University of Chicago Press.

Lee, J. (1989). *Ireland 1912–1985: Politics and Society*. Cambridge: Cambridge University Press.

Leonard, H. (1979). *Home Before Night*. London: Penguin.

Logan, P. (1981). *Irish Folk Medicine*. Belfast: Appletree Press.

Lysaght, P. (1995). 'Visible death: Attitudes to the dying in Ireland', *Marvels and Tales*, 9, pp. 27–59, 87–99.

Lysaght, P. (1998). *A Pocket Book of the Banshee*. Dublin: O'Brien.

Lysaght, P. (2001). 'Lamenting', In G. Howarth and O. Leaman (eds), *Encyclopaedia of Death and Dying* (pp. 280–2). London: Routledge.

Lysaght, P. (2005). Personal communication, 21 November.

MacAdam, R. S. (1858). 'Six hundred Gaelic proverbs collected in Ulster', *Ulster Journal of Archaeology*, 7, pp. 172–83.

MacCana, P. (1980). 'Women in Irish mythology', *The Crane Bag*, 4, pp. 7–11.

MacCoitir, N. (2003). *Irish Trees: Myths, Legends and Folklore*. Cork: Wilton Press.

MacCon Iomaire, L. (1988). *Ireland of the Proverbs*. Dublin: Town House.

MacDonald, T.D. (1926), *Gaelic Proverbs and Proverbial Sayings: With English Translations*. Stirling: E. Mackay.

MacDonald, T. K. and Ross, M. (1999). 'Assessing the accuracy of predictions about dating relationships: How and why do lovers' predictions differ from those made by observers?' *Journal of Personality and Social Psychology*, 54, pp. 21–33.

MacKillop, J. (2001). 'A primer of Irish numbers', in P. Monaghan (ed.), *Irish Spirit*. Dublin: Wolfhound.

McCone, K. (1990). *Pagan Past and Christian Present in Early Irish Literature*. Maynooth: An Sagart/Maynooth.

McCourt, F. (1996). *Angela's Ashes*. London: HarperCollins.

McGahern, J. (2002). *That They May Face the Rising Sun*. London: Faber and Faber.

McGee, M. (2005). *Self-Help, Inc.: Makover Culture in American Life*. Oxford: Oxford University Press.

McLoughlin, D. (1994). 'Women and sexuality in nineteenth century Ireland', *Irish Journal of Psychology*, 15, pp. 266–75.

McNeill. W. (1982). *The Pursuit of Power: Technology, Armed Force and Society Since AD 1000*. Chicago: University of Chicago Press.

McWilliams, B. (1994). *Weather Eye*. Dublin: Lilliput.

McWilliams, B. (1999). 'The kingdom of the air: The progress of meteorology', in J. W. Foster (ed.), *Nature in Ireland: A Scientific and Cultural History* (pp. 115–32). Dublin: Lilliput.

McWilliams, B. (2005a). 'Listen to what the frog has to say', *The Irish Times*, 26 September.

McWilliams, B. (2005b). 'Hunter's moon and Mars in sky tonight', *The Irish Times*, 17 October.

Marx, K. (1976[1849]). *Wage, Labour and Capital*. New York: International
Publishers.

Matarazzo, J. D. (1972). *Wechsler's Measure and Appraisal of Adult
Intelligence* (5th edn). Oxford: Oxford University Press.

Meyer, K. (1906). *The Triads of Ireland. Royal Irish Academy Todd Lecture
Series*, vol. XIII. Dublin: Royal Irish Academy.

Mieder, B., and Mieder, W. (1977). 'Tradition and innovation: Proverbs in
advertising', *Journal of Popular Culture*, *11*, pp. 308–19.

Mieder, W. (1985). 'A proverb is a short sentence of wisdom', *Proverbium*,
2, 109–43.

Mieder, W. (1993). *Proverbs Are Never Out of Season*. New York: Oxford
University Press.

Mieder, W. (1997). *Politics of Proverbs: From Traditional Wisdom to
Proverbial Stereotypes*. Madison WI: University of Wisconsin Press.

Mieder, W. (2004). *Proverbs: A Handbook*. Westport, Ct: Greenwood
Press.

Mieder, W. and Dundes, A. (eds) (1981). *The Wisdom of Many: Essays on the
Proverb*. New York: Garland.

Mieder, W. and Holmes, B. (2000). *Children and Proverbs Speak the Truth:
Teaching Proverbial Wisdom to Fourth Graders*. Burlington, Vermont:
University of Vermont.

Milner, G. (1971). 'The quartered shield: Outline of a semantic taxonomy
of proverbs', in E. Ardener (ed.), *Social Anthropology and Language*
(pp. 243–69). London: Tavistock.

Monaghan, P. (ed.) (2001). *Irish Spirit*. Dublin: Wolfhound.

Morgan, M. and Grube, J. W. (1994). 'The Irish and alcohol: A classic case
of ambivalence', *Irish Journal of Psychology*, *15*, pp. 390–403.

Mullen, B., Rozell, D. and Johnson, C. (2000). 'Ethnophaulisms for ethnic
immigrant groups: Cognitive representations of "the minority"
and "the foreigner"', *Group Processes and Interpersonal Relations*, *3*,
pp. 5–24.

Myers, D. (2002). *Social Psychology* (7th edn). Boston: McGraw-Hill.

Ní Fhloinn, B. (1980). 'Cold iron and the cast: A study of the naming
prejudices of Irish fishermen'. Unpublished master's dissertation,
Department of Irish Folklore, University College Dublin.

Ó Cinnéide, M. (1984). 'Tuartha aimsire i mbealoideas na hÉireann',
Béaloideas, *52*, pp. 35–69.

O'Connor, A. (2003). 'Wakes', in B. Lalor (ed.), *The Encyclopaedia of Ireland* (p. 1116). Dublin: Gill & Macmillan.

O'Farrell, P. (1980). *Gems of Irish Wisdom*. Dublin: Mercier.

O'Farrell, P. (2004). *Irish customs*. Dublin: Gill & Macmillan.

Ó hÓgáin, D. (2002). *Irish Superstitions* (2nd edn). Dublin: Gill & Macmillan.

Orwell, George (1937). *The Road to Wigan Pier*. London: Victor Gollancz.

Ó Súilleabháin, S. (1967). *Irish Wake Amusements*. Dublin: Mercier.

Partridge, A. (1978). *A Hundred Irish Proverbs and Sayings*. Dublin: Folens.

Pasamanick, J. (1983). 'Talk does cook rice: Proverb abstraction through social interaction', *International Journal for the Sociology of Language*, *44*, pp. 5–25.

Peck, J.W. (1978). 'Rats defend different body weights depending on palatability and accessibility of their food', *Journal of Comparative and Physiological Psychology*, *92*, pp. 555–70.

Pennebaker, J. W. (1997). *Opening Up: The Healing Power of Expressing Emotion*. New York: Guilford Press.

Pennebaker, J. W., and Lightner, J. M. (1980). 'Competition of internal and external information in an exercise setting', *Journal of Personality and Social Psychology*, *39*, pp. 165–74.

Piaget, J. (1969). *Language and Thought in the Child*. New York: Basic Books.

Raymond, J. (1956). 'Tension in proverbs: More light on international thinking', *Western Folklore*, *15*, pp. 153–8.

Ridout, R. and Witting, C. (1969). *English Proverbs Explained*. London: Pan Books.

Roback, A. A. (1944). *A Dictionary of International Slurs*. Cambridge: Sci-Art Publishers.

Robinson, F. N. (1945). 'Irish proverbs and Irish national character', *Modern Philology*, *43*, pp. 1–10.

Rogers, T. (1990). 'Proverbs as psychological theories . . . or is it the other way around?', *Canadian Psychology*, *31*, pp. 195–207.

Rosenstock, G. (2000). *Irish Weather Wisdom*. Belfast: Appletree.

Roud, S. (2003). *The Penguin Guide to the Superstitions of Britain and Ireland*. London: Penguin.

Salerno, S. (2005). *Sham: How the Self-Help Movement Made America Helpless*. New York: Random House.

Sayers, P., and Ní Chinnéide, M. (1936). *Peig: A Scéal Féin*. Baile Átha Cliath: Clólucht an Talbóidigh.

Seligman, M. E. P. (1998). *Learned Optimism: How to Change Your Mind and Your Life* (2nd edn). New York: Pocket Books.

Seligman, M. E. P. (2002). *Authentic Happiness: Using the New Positive Psychology to Realize Your Potential for Lasting Fulfilment*. New York: Free Press.

Sheldon, K., Elliot, A. J., Youngmee, K. and Kasser, T. (2001). 'What is satisfying about satisfying events? Testing 10 candidate psychological needs', *Journal of Personality and Social Psychology*, 80, pp. 325–39.

Siegelman, L. (1981). 'Is ignorance bliss? A reconsideration of the folk wisdom. *Human Relations, 34*, pp. 965–74.

Simons, P. (2005a). 'Nutkins may not be so clever', *The Times*, 25 October, p. 71.

Simons, P. (2005b). 'St Jude brings feast of stormy weather', *The Times*, 28 October, p. 86.

Simpson, J. A., and Speake, J. (eds, 1993). *The Concise Oxford English Dictionary of Proverbs*. Oxford: Oxford University Press.

Sowell, T. (1996). *Migrations and Cultures*. New York: Basic Books.

Stanovich, K. (2004). *How To Think Straight About Psychology* (7th edn). Boston, MA: Allyn & Bacon.

Teigen, K. H. (1986). 'Old truths or fresh insights? A study of students' evaluations of proverbs', *British Journal of Social Psychology*, 25, pp. 43–9.

Van Lancker, D. R. (1990). 'The neurology of proverbs', *Behavioural Neurology, 3*, pp. 169–87.

Warnes, H. H. (1979). 'Cultural factors in Irish psychiatry', *Psychiatric Journal of the University of Ottawa, 4*, pp. 329–35.

Whiting, B.J. (1952). 'Proverbs and proverbial sayings: Introduction', in *The Frank C. Brown Collection of North Carolina Folklore*, vol. 1 (Durham: North Carolina).

Whiting, B. J. (1989). *Modern Proverbs and Proverbial Sayings*. Cambridge, MA: Harvard University Press.

Williams, F. (1988). 'Triads and other enumerative proverbs from South Ulster', Ulster *Folklife, 34*, pp. 60–7.

Williams, F. (1992). *Irish Proverbs*. Dublin: Poolbeg.

Williams, F. (1995). 'Six hundred Gaelic proverbs collected in Ulster by Robert McCrum', *Proverbium*, *12*, pp. 343–55.

Williams, F. (2003). *Wellerisms in Ireland : Towards a Corpus from Oral and Literary Sources*. Burlington: University of Vermont.

Zajonc, R. B. (1968). 'Attitudinal effects of mere exposure', *Journal of Personality and Social Psychology*, *Monograph Supplement*, *9*, pp. 1–21.

Index of Proverbs

Note: All proverbs cited in the text are listed alphabetically under separate headings: 'English language proverbs', 'Irish language proverbs' and 'French language proverbs'. Proverbs in the last two sections are accompanied by English translations and are only repeated in the first section where circumstances require it. Page references in *italics* indicate illustrations

ENGLISH–LANGUAGE PROVERBS

IRISH-LANGUAGE PROVERBS

FRENCH-LANGUAGE PROVERBS

General Index

Berkowitz, L. 88
Bernstein, D. A. 39
Berreby, D. 134
bias 126
'big wind' (1839) 60, 75
bird market (Dublin) 85
Birnbaum, J. A. 9
Bloom, Leopold 95
Book of Proverbs xi
Book of Wisdom 141–2
Bord na Gaeilge 22
Bourke, Austin 59
brain dysfunction 9
Brickman, Philip 89
Brigid, Saint 68
Britain 78–9, 103, 122–3
Bush, George W. 133
buttermilk 41
Buunk, B. P. 126

Cambray Homily 136–7
Campbell, Donald 89
capitalism 36
Cara matches 22
Carcur, Co. Wexford 149
Carndonagh Cross, Co. Donegal 105
Carr, P. 60
Cash, T. F. 12
Cashman, S. 15, 29, 45, 47, 48, 51, 52, 53, 80, 81, 82, 83, 87, 118–19, 121, 128, 130, 144
Castlegal, Co. Sligo 23
categorisation 134
Catholic Irish Alcoholism 53
Catholicism 36

cats 151
caution 121
Ceathru Rua (Carraroe) Co. Galway, 145
Celtic spirituality 31
Celtic Tiger 43
Celts 29, 139–40
cereals 41
ceremonial role xii
certainty/uncertainty 124
Cervantes, Miguel de 3
Chant of Jimmie Blacksmith, The (Keneally) 55
chastity 120
children 7–8, 24, 44
Christianity 110–11, 112, 140–1
class resentment, 52
classification 134–5, 151
climate 59–61; see also weather lore
Clogher, Co. Louth 129
combativeness 32
Comhdhail Naisunta na Gaeilge 22
common sense 1, 11
Concise Oxford English Dictionary of Proverbs (Simpson and Speake) 122, 124
Connemara 24
Connolly, S. J. 40, 41
conquest 33
consequences 124
consumption, 40, 43, 124; see also alcohol; food and drink
contentment 150
contextual influences 11
Corleck, Co. Cavan 139
Cormac Mac Airt 28

religion 108, 121; *see also*
  Christianity
repetitive elements 6
rhyme 4, 26
Ridout, R. 3
Rising Sun (fishing vessel) 102–3
Road to Wigan Pier, The (Orwell) 88
Roback, A. A. 9, 134
Robbins, Anthony, 7
Robinson, F. N. 31–3
Rogers, T. 7, 11
Romans 54, 55, 62, 63
Rosenstock, G. 63, 74
Ross, M. 126
Roud, S. 64, 139, 140, 141, 146
Rozell, D. 9
Russell, Lord John 3

St Brigid's Day 68
St John's Night 140
St Patrick's Day 68
St Patrick's Pilgrimage 69
St Swithin's Day 68, 70
saints' days 68
Salerno, S. 7
Saltee Islands, Co. Wexford 102
same-sex unions 130
Sayers, Peig 95, 103, 116
Scandinavian folklore 32
schizophrenia 9
schools 30
Schools' Collection (Irish Folklore
  Commission) 28
Scotland 66, 70
Scottish colonisation 41
sea 102–3
Seabhac, An 15

Sean-Fhocla Chonnacht 28
seanfhocail 21
Seanfhocail na Mumhan 28
Seanfhocail Uladh 28
self-disclosure 12
self-help movement 7
Seligman, M. E. P. 98
sexism 127–8
sexuality 115, 120
Shakespeare, William 139
shamrock 140
Shane (film) 17
Sheldon, Kenneth 88
Sheridan, Philip Henry 9
sidh 104
Siegelman, L. 12
silence 135
Simons, P. 61, 68
Simpson, J. A. 122, 124
Six Hundred Gaelic Proverbs
  (MacAdam) 30
Sixguns and Society (Wright) 17
size 124
sleep 99–100
slogans 6–7
smoking ban 44
social change 33, 35–7, 92
social loafing 14
Solomon xi
Soviet Russia 5
Sowell, T. 79
Speake, J. 122, 124
Stanovich, K. 10, 11
Steen, F. xiii
stout 43
stress 98–9
stylistic devices 25–6